THE MEXICAN KITCHEN

With Rod Santana

Published by: KMBH-TV
                   P.O. Box 2147
                   Harlingen, Texas 78551

ISBN: 0-9636763-0-X

Table Of Contents

PREFACE

South Texas was a part of Mexico or New Spain for several centuries before the area became part of the United States in 1848. More than 80% of the residents of the Lower Rio Grande Valley, where KMBH-TV broadcasts, are Hispanic. Our coverage area also includes Matamoros and Reynosa, Mexico.

Due to our proximity to Mexico and the close cultural ties the population has to Mexico, it should be no surprise that assembling recipes for our cookbook and companion television series was not difficult. However, determining which recipes to use proved to be a formidable task.

Through the efforts of our Editorial Review Committee, who are the real experts, we chose to present the following. Recipes were gathered from numerous Valley residents. Many also came from research we conducted within Mexico while producing a travel series and an instructional television series about the country.

We are proud of the results of our work and hope that you enjoy preparing these as much as we have in assembling them.

Darrell Rowlett
Jozi Maldonado
Executives Producers
TheMexican Kitchen
with Rod Santana

KMBH-TV
Harlingen, Texas

UTENSILS

One can make wonderful Mexican dishes without purchasing a great many new utensils. However, there are a few relatively inexpensive tools that will greatly enhance whatever you prepare.

Comal

This utensil is a cast iron griddle. Many are made to fit over the eye of an electric or gas stove. There is also a version available that fits over two eyes. The *comal* is primarily used to make tortillas.

Molcajete and Tejolote

Cooking Mexican dishes often requires the use of a mortar and pestle to grind salsa ingredients. An authentic *molcajete* and *tejolote* is made of black basalt (volcanic rock). The *molcajete* is normally about eight inches in diameter and supported by three legs, although they can be found in different sizes. It often also doubles as a salsa serving dish after a sauce is made. The *tejolote* is usually about two inches in diameter and four inches long. A new *molcajete* is usually "cured" by grinding dry rice into it and rinsing several times.

Olla

This is a traditional clay pot for making beans.

Tortilla Press

It is much easier to use a press to make the tortillas round than to attempt to pat them out by hand.

TORTILLAS

The basic grain that native Americans used in what is now Mexico for thousands of years was *maize* or corn. Along with chilies, beans, tomatoes, and fresh fruits, the early people developed a cuisine all their own.

At Mexican style restaurants in the United States, the flour *tortilla* is more generally served, but within Mexico, the corn tortilla is a staple with almost any meal. One reason is that many wheat products must be imported and the wheat or flour *tortilla* is a post-Hispanic bread. Also, the interior has more Indian influence than northern Mexico. Wheat was a Spanish staple.

The *tortilla* is a simple blanket that can be wrapped around almost any food. It may also be used in place of a spoon or fork by dipping up the food from the plate. This was a common use of bread by the Spanish when they settled Mexico and was also a practice of the Native Americans.

Throughout Mexico and North America, the basic tortilla of the Native Americans can be filled with cheese and it becomes a *quesadilla* or an *enchilada*. Fill it with meat and it's a *taco*. *Chalupas* are *tortillas* that are fried whole. Cut it up in small pieces and fry it and you have chips or *tostadas*. But regardless of how it is cooked or what meat or vegetable is used, the tortilla is normally a basic ingredient.

CHILIES (PEPPERS)

Most Mexican dishes include fresh tomatoes, some type of chili pepper, and one form or another of the *tortilla.* Green chilies are normally served fresh and red chilies, which are ripened chilies, are almost always dried and ground before using.

Although there are hundreds of varieties of chilies, there are three varieties that are most often used in this book: serranos, jalapenos, and poblanos.

The serrano is a small green chili, usually about 1 to 1 1/2 inches long, whose seeds and veins are very hot. They can be used fresh or roasted and can be found in most large grocery stores.

The jalapeno is a slightly larger dark green chili whose seeds and veins can be very hot. They are canned and available in virtually any grocery.

The poblano vary in shape, color and size. They are generally triangular in shape and are somewhat larger than the serrano or jalapeno. Depending where a traveler might be in Mexico, the chilies have several different names. They are normally roasted and peeled before using.

ONIONS

The Spanish Onion is common and versatile. Purple Salad Onions may be used raw on salads. White Burmuda Onions also used for salads or eaten raw. The Yellow Onion is quite popular and most versatile. The 1015 Onion is a sweet, South-Texas favorite.

GARLIC

We could not imagine Mexican food without this common foodstuff. There is no substitute for the real thing. Garlic powder or garlic salt just are not the same. Grinding it in a *molcajete* may seem like a chore, but your tastebuds will know the difference, or you can try a garlic press.

If you are purchasing garlic in the supermarket, find a full head since they are placed in cold storage and have probably dried out. To store parts of garlic, leave out at room temperature, do not refrigerate.

To clean garlic, crush the entire head in the palm of your hand so that the cloves fall apart. Select a clove and crush with flat side of knife. The dry peel will separate from the clove. Now you are ready to grind the cloves and other spices. Once you have mashed all the spices to a paste, fill the *molcajete* with water and pour the mixture in your dish.

APPETIZERS

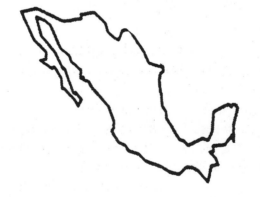

Tex Mex Stuffed Peppers

Chiles Rellenos

8 large poblano peppers or 8 small green peppers*
16 ounces Monterrey Jack or cheddar cheese
8 egg yolks
2 tablespoons water
1/4 cup all purpose flour
1/2 teapoon salt
8 egg whites
Cooking oil
Red chili sauce (see recipe)

Broil peppers 2 inches from heat for 15 minutes, turning often, until all sides are blistered. Place peppers in a bag; close bag and let stand about 10 minutes or until cool enough to handle. Peel peppers, removing stems and seeds. Cut cheese into 8 pieces to fit peppers. Stuff each pepper with a piece of cheese. Set aside. In small mixer bowl beat egg yolks and water slightly. Add flour and salt. Beat on high speed about 6 minutes or until thick and lemon colored. Beat egg whites until stiff peaks form. Fold yolks into whites. Heat 1/2 inch of oil to 375 degrees. Spoon about 1/3 cup batter in a circle a little larger than the pepper. As batter begins to set, gently top mound of batter with a stuffed pepper. Cover with another 1/3 cup batter. Continue cooking 2 to 3 minutes or until underside is browned. Turn carefully; brown second side. Drain on paper towel; keep warm on baking sheet in 300 degree oven while preparing remaining peppers. Serve with red chili sauce, if desired.

*Poblano chili peppers are similar in taste but slightly smaller than bell peppers and have a pointed tip.

Serves 8

Mexican Flaming Cheese

Queso Flameado a La Mexicana

1 link of Mexican sausage (Chorizo)
16 ounces of cheese (White, Cheddar, or Monterrey Jack), grated
Flour or corn tortillas

Brown sausage in a skillet and drain. Using a microwave-safe dish place cheese in the dish. Heat until melted. Take the cheese out and add the sausage in the middle of the cheese dish. Serve hot with warm tortillas.

Serves 3-4

Flaming Cheese

Queso Flameado

*16 ounces of Mexican white cheese of choice ***
18 wheat or corn tortillas

The cheese should be sliced in thin strips and layered in a shallow, flame proof dish. The cheese can be melted on the stove top or in the oven. Serve immediately with warm tortillas and the tomato/chili sauce of your choice.

* If unavailable in your market, substitute Monterrey Jack.

Serves 6

Nachos

6 corn tortillas
Cooking oil
8 ounces cheese
Jalapenos

Cut fresh tortillas into quarters and deep-fry or bake until crisp. Place nacho wedges on a cookie sheet and cover with cheese. Garnish with small slices of jalapenos. Heat until melted. Excellent to serve with dips.

*To make Panchos, simply add refried beans on the chips before the cheese.

Serves 3

5

Nachos Deluxe

1 package of corn tortillas or restaurant style nacho chips
2 cups of refried beans
1 pound of cheese (Cheddar or Monterrey Jack)
Oil for frying

Optional:
Lettuce, chopped
Tomato, chopped
Picante sauce

If frying your chips, cut corn tortillas in quarters. Fry corn tortillas in hot oil until crisp. If not, place restaurant style chips on cookie sheet, spread beans on chips. If using cheese slices, cut triangles and place one on each chip. If using grated cheese, sprinkle cheese on chips. Put in 350 degree oven until cheese melts. Add lettuce, tomato, and picante sauce, if desired.

Serves 6-7

Panchos Deluxe

6 corn tortillas
1/2 cup refried beans
3/4 cups green chili sauce
Guacamole (see recipe)
Vegetable oil
1 cup (4 ounces) shredded sharp cheese

Quarter each tortilla. Deep-fry or bake tortilla wedges until lightly browned and crisp. Spread each tortilla wedge with refried beans; sprinkle with cheese. Top each with green chili sauce. Heat until melted. Top each nacho with guacamole to serve. Makes 3 dozen appetizers.

*Chips can also be baked.

Serves 4-6

Mexican Corn Dog

8-10 frankfurters
8-10 corn tortillas
Toothpicks
Oil to fry

Heat oil in pan or deep-fry. Soften tortillas in oil. Roll a frankfurter in a tortilla.; place toothpick to hold tortillas closed. Put in hot oil or deep-fry until crispy and toasted on all sides. Drain on paper towels. Remove toothpick. Dip in mustard if you like.

Serves 5

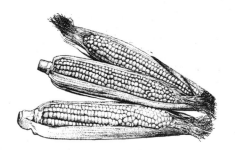

Stuffed Jalapeno Peppers

Jalapenos Rellenos

1 dozen Jalapenos
8 ounces cream cheese
1 egg
1 cup milk
Salt to taste
Pepper to taste
Flour
Bread Crumbs

Split jalapenos in half and remove seeds. Place 1/4 of removed seeds in bowl and mix with cream cheese; stuff peppers and place in freezer until frozen. Prepare egg mixture using 1 egg and 1 cup milk with salt and pepper to taste, per 1 dozen jalapenos. When peppers are frozen, roll in plain flour, dip in egg mixture, roll in bread crumbs, again in egg mixture and again in breadcrumbs, pressing firmly and return to freezer until ready to use. Deep fry at 325 degrees until brown. Serve hot.

Serves 6-8

Slivered Peppers with Mushrooms

Rajas con Champinones

2 cups fresh mushrooms, sliced
8 jalapenos, sliced and deveined
1 onion, sliced
4 cloves garlic, finely chopped
1 sprig goosefoot, finely chopped (see glossary)
2 tablespoons oil
Salt to taste

Cook mushrooms over low heat for ten minutes. Add salt to taste. Add oil and stir-fry remaining ingredients. Serve on hot corn tortillas.

Yield: 2 cups

Shrimp Ranchero

Camarones Rancheros

2 tablespoons oil
1 onion, sliced
3-4 serrano peppers, chopped
1 1/2 cups tomato, chopped
3 cloves of garlic, mashed
1/4 cup coriander
1 cup water
1 pound shrimp, peeled and deveined

Saute onion in oil; add pepper, tomato, garlic, coriander and water. Bring to a boil; add shrimp and simmer for 10-12 minutes.

Yield: 4-5 cups

Red Snapper Fritters

1 or more pounds of red snapper
2 eggs
4 1/2 ounces flour
4 1/2 ounces butter
4 1/2 ounces bread crumbs
1 lemon
1 cup milk
1 small onion
2 cloves garlic
1 teaspoon parsley
Oil
Pepper
Salt

Place washed fish into boiling water with onion, juice from 1/2 lemon, garlic and parsley. Melt butter in a saucepan. Add flour and cook until brown. Pour in the fish broth. Stir until the mixture thickens into a dough. Add the other 1/2 of the lemon juice, salt and pepper. Remove from heat, shred the fish and add to the dough. Allow it to cool. Beat the eggs and add to cool dough. Form small balls, dip in eggs and cover with bread crumbs. Fry in oil.

Serves 4

Fish Salad

Ceviche

1 1/2 pounds fresh flounder, sole, or other firm white fish fillets
3/4 cup fresh lime or lemon juice to cover
Salt
Celery salt
Pepper
3 medium size scallions
3 medium size tomatoes, peeled, seeded and cubed
2 ounce jar pimiento strips, drained
1/2 cup olive oil
3 tablespoons wine vinegar
2 tablespoons finely minced coriander
3/4 teaspoon oregano
1/2 teaspoon ground cumin
2 teaspoons finely minced fresh serrano peppers

Cut fish into 1/2 inch cubes. Place in a bowl with lime juice covering fish. Chill overnight. Drain and wash fish under cold water. Drain well and pat fish dry with paper towels. Sprinkle generously with salt, celery salt and pepper. Cut scallions (white and solid part of green) lengthwise in half. Cut crosswise into 1/4 inch slices. In mixing bowl, combine fish with remaining ingredients. Toss well. Marinate 4 to 6 hours. Serve with crackers or tortilla chips.

Serves 4-6

Fish in Lime Juice

Ceviche

1 pound firm white fish fillets
7-8 large limes
12 ounces diced, boiled tomatoes
4 serrano peppers
1/2 teaspoon oregano
Salt and pepper to taste

Cube the fish in small pieces and squeeze the limes over them in a bowl. Cover and allow to soak in the refrigerator for at least four hours. Stir every half hour. After marinating, add the tomatoes and peppers. Mix, cover and allow to cool in the refrigerator for an hour more. Can be served with avocado slices on the side.

Serves 2

Steamed Squash

Calabazitas al Vapor

1/2 squash
1/2 stick margarine
2 teaspoons finely chopped parsley
1/4 cup chopped onion
1 cup grated cheese
Salt
Pepper

Wash and slice squash. In a skillet, heat the squash to a boil. Add the butter, parsley and onion. Simmer on low heat until almost all the water is gone or squash is tender. Add the salt and pepper and sprinkle with cheese.

Serves 2

DIPS AND SAUCES

Shrimp Canapes

Camarones Rancheros

1 pound cooked shrimp
1 tablespoon chili powder
1/4 cup finely minced water chestnuts
1 1/2 tablespoons minced onion
1 hard-boiled egg, minced
3 ounces softened cream cheese
Dash of salt and pepper
Dash of hot pepper seasoning
1 teaspoon lemon juice
Minced parsley
Worcestershire sauce, to taste

Combine all ingredients and adjust seasoning. Chill thoroughly. Spread onto Melba toast rounds or toast. Garnish with parsley.

Yield: 3 cups

Mexican Bean Dip

1 pound pinto beans
5 cups water
2 cups chopped onion
1/2 (6 0z) can tomato paste
3 jalapeno peppers
1 tablespoon bacon drippings
1/2 teaspoon powdered onion
Pinch of cumin
2 teaspoons chili powder
1/2 tablespoon oregano
1/2 cup butter
1/2 cup grated sharp cheese
Optional:
2 bay leaves

Bean recipe: Soak beans. Drain and add more water, onion, tomato paste, peppers, drippings, bay leaves and cumin. Cook slowly until beans are very soft. If the dip is too dry, always add hot water, never cold..

Dip recipe: Mix chili powder and oregano with enough water to make paste. Add to beans. Mash beans through strainer. Add butter, cheese and 1/2 teaspoon salt. Blend all ingredients to a paste. Heat prior to serving. Serve with corn chips.

Yield: 4 cups

Bean Dip

1 cup cooked pinto beans, drained
1 teaspoon chili powder
1/8 teaspoon ground cumin
1 tablespoon dry taco or fajita seasoning
1/4 cup sour cream
2-4 tablespoons picante sauce
1/8 teaspoon garlic powder
1/2 cup processed cheese, shredded or cubed
Corn chips

In a blender or food processor, place all ingredients and blend at high speed until smooth.

Yield: 2 1/2 cups

Tillie's Special Dip

2 (9 ounce) cans bean dip or 1 1/2 cans spicy refried beans
3 mashed avocados
2 tablespoons lemon juice
1/2 pint sour cream
1/2 cup mayonnaise
1 package taco seasoning mix
2 small cans black olives
3 firm tomatoes, diced
8 ounces shredded cheddar cheese
Tortilla chips

Layer as follows in a large serving dish:

Mix bean dip, avocados and lemon juice for first layer. Mix sour cream, mayonnaise and taco seasoning mix together and spread over first layer. Sprinkle the cheddar over this and decorate with sliced tomatoes and olives. Serve with tortilla chips.

Yield: 5-6 cups

Avocado Deluxe Dip

2 avocados
1/4 cup onion, finely chopped
1 teaspoon chili powder*
1 medium tomato, chopped
1 tablespoon lemon juice
1 tablespoon salt
Optional:
Salt to taste
6 crispy cooked bacon slices, crumbled
3 ounce package cream cheese, softened
1/4 cup green onion slices (to replace onion)
1/2 cup ripe olive slices
1/2 cup sour cream

Combine all ingredients in small mixing bowl; blend well.

*The chili powder can be deleted.

Yield: 2 cups

Avocado Dip

Guacamole

1/2 cup chopped onion
2 serrano peppers
3-4 sprigs of coriander
Salt to taste
2 avocados
1 large tomato, skinned and cubed

Grind 1/4 cup of onion, peppers, 2 sprigs of coriander and salt to a smooth paste. Halve the avocado, scoop out the fruit, and save the seeds. Add the avocado fruit to the seasoning and grind to a smooth paste. Add the tomato, 1/4 cup of onion and remaining chopped coriander. Mix and serve with chips.

To keep the dip fresh, add a squeeze of lemon and return the avocado seeds to the mixture until ready to serve.

Yield: 1 1/2 cups

Taco Deluxe Dip

3 mashed avocados
1/2 pint sour cream
1 package guacamole seasoning mix
3 tomatoes, chopped
1 1/2 cups refried beans
Green or black olives, to taste
4 ounces shredded Monterrey Jack cheese
4 ounces shredded cheddar cheese
1 bag of corn tortilla chips or fried corn tortillas

Mix avocados, sour cream and seasoning mix. Then mix in tomatoes and olives. Spread refried beans evenly on chips. Top with avocado mixture. Sprinkle cheese over top.

Yield: 5-6 cups

Shrimp and Avocado Dip

Campechano

5 diced avocados
7 diced tomatoes
1 pound boiled and cut shrimp
5 chopped green onions with tops
1 bunch of coriander
10 limes
2 garlic cloves, crushed
Salt
Pepper
Corn tortillas

Mix avocados, onion, garlic and tomatoes. Add the peeled, deveined, and cut-up shrimp and chopped coriander. Mix well. Squeeze juice from limes and mix in salt and pepper. Stir to combine ingredients well. Serve with warm tortillas.

Yield: 10 cups

Super Chili Dip

Chili con Queso

2 tablespoons butter
1/4 cup onion, finely chopped
1 (14 1/2 ounce) can tomatoes, drained
1 (4 ounce) can green chili peppers, drained and chopped
1/4 teaspoon salt
3 cloves garlic, crushed
1 tablespoon Worcestershire sauce
1/4 cup heavy cream or evaporated milk
1 pound American cheese
1/2 pound cheddar cheese
Corn tortilla chips

In a medium skillet, saute onions in butter until tender. Add tomatoes, peppers, salt, garlic and Worcestershire sauce. Simmer for 10 minutes. Pour into a double boiler, add cheese that has been cut up into small pieces and stir until cheese melts. Add the cream and cook over boiling water for 30 minutes. Serve with corn tortilla chips.

Yield: 5-6 cups

Chili and Cheese Dip

Chili con Queso

1/2 cup onion, finely chopped
1 tablespoon butter or margarine
2 medium tomatoes, peeled, seeded and chopped
1 (4 ounce) can green chili peppers, rinsed, seeded and chopped
1/4 teaspoon salt
Several drops bottled hot pepper sauce
1 1/2 cups shredded cheddar cheese
Corn tortilla chips
Optional:
Milk*

In medium skillet cook onion in butter or margarine until tender, but not brown. Stir in tomatoes, peppers, salt and pepper sauce. Simmer, uncovered, for 10 minutes. Add cheese, a little at a time, stirring until cheese is melted. Stir in a little milk if mixture becomes too thick. Transfer to fondue pot; keep warm over low heat during serving. Serve immediately with corn tortilla chips.

*If the mixture is too thick, milk can be added.

Yield: 1 3/4 cups

Chili and Cheese Dip

Chili con Queso

1 medium onion, chopped
10 ounces cheddar cheese
6-8 tablespoons picante sauce
2 tablespoons butter/margarine
6 ounces American cheese, cubed
*1 (15 ounce) can chili (no beans)**

Saute onion in butter until soft. Add cheeses and cook over low heat until melted, stirring occasionally. Stir in picante sauce, then add chili. Serve with chips.

*See recipe for chili if homemade chili is desired.

Serves 8

Chili Dip Ole

Chili con Carne

1/2 pound ground beef
1 large onion, finely chopped
1 (1 1/4 ounces) chili seasoning mix
1 (6 ounce) can tomato paste
Corn chips
Optional:
1 tablespoon sugar

Crumble ground beef in medium skillet. Stir in onions. Cook until beef is browned. Drain. Stir in chili seasoning, tomato paste and sugar. Cook at high 3 to 4 minutes. Serve warm with corn chips.

Yield: 2 cups

Cucumber-Garlic Dip

1 medium cucumber, peeled and finely chopped
1/2 pound Mexican or feta cheese, crumbled
1/2 cup green onions, thinly sliced
1/2 cup mayonnaise
1/2 cup plain yogurt
1 teaspoon oregano
3 tablespoons parsley, fresh or dry
3 garlic cloves, peeled and crushed

In a medium bowl, combine all ingredients and mix well. Refrigerate 2 hours before serving.

Yield: 3 cups

Green Sauce

Salsa Verde

2 pounds tomatillos, sliced (see glossary)
1 tablespoon chopped onion
1/2 teaspoon garlic, chopped
1 teaspoon salt
1/2 tablespoon butter
1/2 cup water

Fry onion and garlic in butter lightly. Add *tomatillos,* salt and water. Simmer for 20 to 30 minutes or until *tomatillos* are soft. Stir thoroughly until blended. Do not use electric blender as the *tomatillos* will foam!

Yield: 2 cups

Enchilada Sauce

Salsa para Enchiladas

3 tablespoons shortening
3 tablespoons flour
3 tablespoons chili powder
3/4 teaspoon salt
2 cups water
1 can tomatoes with green peppers

Melt shortening over low heat; stir in the flour, salt and chili powder. Continue stirring for a few minutes. Remove from heat and add water and tomatoes. Place back on burner and continue stirring until smooth. Let simmer for 20 minutes. Add more water occasionally if sauce becomes too thick, but sauce should be slightly watery. Top any style enchilada with this sauce.

The secret to making any gravy is to always remove from heat before adding liquids.

Yield: 3 1/2 cups

Cheese Sauce

Salsa de Queso

1 teaspoon oil
1 chopped onion
1 cup American cheese, cubed or grated
1-2 chopped tomatoes
3/4 cup water
Optional:
1-2 jalapenos, chopped

Saute onion in oil. Add cheese, tomatoes and jalapenos. When cheese begins to melt, add water. Simmer 4-6 minutes until smooth.

Yield: 2 cups

Mexican Hot Sauce

Salsa Mexicana

1 garlic clove, crushed
3 jalapeno peppers
1/2 teaspoon cumin
1/2 teaspoon salt
Pepper to taste
1 (16 ounce) can boiled tomatoes

Combine garlic, cumin, salt, jalapenos and juice from the tomatoes in a blender and blend for about half a minute on high. Add the tomato meat and blend on low a few seconds to achieve a consistency. Chill in glass jar.

Yield: 2 cups

Cooked Hot Sauce

Salsa Guisada con Jalapenos

2 cups chopped tomato
1 small onion diced
2-6 fresh serrano or jalapeno peppers, chopped
1/4 cup coriander, chopped
1/2 tablespoon oil
Salt to taste

Saute onion in oil; add remaining ingredients. Bring to a boil and simmer 5-6 minutes. (This salsa may be used for huevos rancheros by pouring on to over-easy eggs.)

Yield: 2 cups

Jalapeno Relish

Salsa Guisada

1/2 cup minced onion
1 teaspoon very finely minced garlic
2 tablespoons peanut oil
1 cup fresh tomatoes, peeled, seeded and cubed
1/4 cup finely minced canned jalapeno peppers
1/4 cup vinegar
Salt

Saute onions and garlic in oil until onions are tender. Add tomatoes, chili peppers and vinegar. Simmer slowly 10 minutes. Season with salt. Cover and chill overnight. Serve with entree.

Yield: 1 1/2 cups

Mild Pepper Sauce

Salsa

1/4 cup white vinegar
2 tablespoons vegetable oil
2 teaspoons sugar
1/4 teaspoon salt
1/4 teaspoon pepper
1 medium size sweet red pepper, diced
1 medium size sweet yellow pepper, diced
1 medium size bell pepper, diced
2 tablespoons chopped parsley

Combine first 5 ingredients in a small saucepan; bring to a boil, stirring until sugar dissolves. Remove from heat. Combine peppers and parsley in a glass bowl; add hot vinegar mixture and stir gently. Cool. Cover and chill. Serve with pork or ham entree.

Yield: 1 2/3 cups

Creamy Green Sauce

Salsa Verde de Crema

1/2 cup sour cream
1/3 cup mayonnaise or salad dressing
1/3 to 1/2 cup green sauce (see recipe)
1 tablespoon lemon juice
1/8 teaspoon chili powder

Combine all ingredients; chill.

Yield: 1 1/4 cups

Basic Red Sauce

4 to 6 dried red ancho peppers
2 cups water

Remove stems and seeds from peppers. Wash peppers and place in sauce pan with water. Bring to boil; simmer for 15 minutes. Set aside covered for 1 hour. Pour in blender or run through colander. This sauce is used for enchiladas or meat stews.

Yield: 2 cups

Garden Fresh Hot Sauce

Salsa Fresca

2 cups tomato, chopped
1 small onion, diced
2-6 fresh serrano or jalapeno peppers, chopped
1/4 cup coriander, chopped
Lemon juice
Salt to taste

Combine all ingredients and serve with chips or as accompaniment to any entree recipe in book.

Yield: 2 cups

Garden Style Picante

Dana's Pico de Gallo

6 firm tomatoes
2 medium onions
1 large avocado
Salt and pepper to taste
2-4 serrano peppers
1 bunch coriander
1/3 cup Italian dressing
Juice from 2 limes
Corn tortilla chips

Chop onions, tomatoes, avocados and peppers. Chop and combine. Leave avocado seeds in mixture. Mince coriander and add to mixture. Add lime juice, dressing, salt and pepper to taste. Chill one hour before serving. Remove seeds prior to serving. Use on chips or as seasoning on Mexican entree.

Yield: 5-7 cups

Garden Style Picante

Pico de Gallo

1 small onion, chopped
1 tomato, peeled and chopped
1 pequin or serrano pepper, finely chopped
1 tablespoon olive oil
2 drops lemon juice or vinegar
Optional:
10 sprigs of coriander

Mix the onion, tomato and pepper together. Add cooking oil and lemon juice. Serve hot or cold with flour tortillas. Flavor develops if it is refrigerated for at least one hour.

Yield: 2 cups

Sauce with Sausage Bits

Salsa Guisada con Chorizo

1/2 small link of Mexican sausage
1/2 small onion
2-3 chopped jalapenos
3 tomatoes
Salt to taste
1 tablespoon butter
1/2 cup water

Chop onion, peppers, and tomatoes. Brown sausage. Saute onion and peppers in butter until onions are translucent; add tomatoes. Salt to taste. Add 1/2 cup water, let simmer on medium until water is cooked off to your desire. This sauce tastes great on any style egg. Use on any Mexican entree.

Yield: 1 cup

Sweet Sauce

Salsa Dulce

1 tablespoon oil
1 bell pepper, chopped
1 onion, chopped
1 large tomato, chopped
1 cup water
Salt to taste

Place oil in medium skillet and saute bell pepper and onion. When onions become translucent, add tomato and water. Simmer for 5 to 10 minutes.

Yield: 1 1/2 cups

Tex-Mex Barbecue Sauce and Marinade

3 tablespoons apple cider vinegar
1 tablespoon vegetable oil
2 teaspoons Worcestershire sauce
1 1/2 teaspoons prepared mustard
1 1/2 teaspoons salt
3/4 cup water
1 (6 ounce can) tomato paste
1/3 cup loosely packed parsley leaves
1/4 cup chopped onion
1 large clove garlic
1/4 cup firmly packed dark brown sugar

In blender container or food processor fitted with metal blade, combine water, tomato paste, parsley, onion, garlic, sugar, vinegar, oil, Worcestershire sauce, mustard and salt. Blend until smooth. To use as a basting sauce, grill 2 pounds of chicken, turkey, meat or fish until at least half done before brushing with sauce. Serve any remaining sauce as a table condiment.

Yield: 2 cups

Lime Vinaigrette

1/4 cup olive oil
2 tablespoons lime juice
2 tablespoons white wine vinegar
1 tablespoon minced onion
1 teaspoon minced coriander or parsley
3/4 teaspoon salt
1/2 teaspoon oregano leaves, crushed
1/2 teaspoon sugar

Combine ingredients; mix well.

Yield: 1/2 cup

Seafood Cocktail Sauce

1 cup jalapeno sauce
1 tablespoon grated onion
1 tablespoon lemon juice
1 tablespoon soy sauce
1 tablespoon horseradish

Mix together and chill. Serve over boiled shrimp or fresh oysters.

Yield: 2 cups

SOUPS - CHILI

Bean Soup

Sopa de Frijol

2 cups cooked beans
2 tomatoes, cubed
1/4 onion, cubed
1 clove garlic, crushed
Salt and pepper to taste
Oil to fry
1 sprig coriander
4 cups water
1/2 cube of chicken boullion
1/2 cup white Mexican cheese

Mash beans or leave them whole in their own juice. In a blender, add tomatoes, onion, garlic, salt and pepper. Blend. Heat this mixture in a skillet with some oil. Add coriander. Add beans, 4 cups water and chicken boullion. Simmer for 20 minutes. Add cheese and serve.

Serves 2-4

Black Bean Soup

Sopa de Frijoles Negros

1 cup black beans
3 tablespoons butter or bacon fat
1 piece celery, diced
1 onion, diced
1 small green pepper, diced
1 clove garlic, crushed
2 tablespoons flour
1 large potato, diced
1 1/2 quarts soup stock
1 cup tomato juice
Salt
Pepper
1 hard-boiled egg
Thin slices of lemon
4 sliced frankfurters*
Optional:
1/4 cup dry sherry or 3 tablespoons bourbon

Wash beans in tap water. Drain. Cover with 3 cups water and soak 1-2 hours. In a heavy soup pot melt butter or fat. Saute onion, celery, green pepper and garlic. Stir in flour. Add the beans, together with the water in which they were soaked. Add potato, soup stock and tomato juice. Bring to a boil. Skim well. Simmer until beans are tender, about 2 to 2 1/2 hours. Stir soup occasionally to keep beans from sticking to pot. Puree the soup in an electric blender. Add sherry or bourbon, if desired. Season with salt and pepper.

If soup is too thick, thin with additional stock. Finely chop hard-boiled egg. Pour soup into bowls. Sprinkle with egg. On each portion float a slice of lemon.

To eliminate soaking beans overnight, bring beans and water to a boil. Boil 2 minutes. Let stand 1 hour. Cook as directed. Frankfurters may be added to the soup in place of the chopped hard-boiled egg.

*Bacon can be substituted for frankfurters.

Serves 4

Clear Soup

Caldo Colado

1 1/2 pounds of lamb backbone
2 quarts water
1 1/2 teaspoons salt
1 chopped onion, browned
1 cup dry bread crumbs
1 pinch oregano
1 serrano chili pulp
1/2 tablespoon chili powder

Put lamb, tap water, chopped onion and salt into large pot and cook on low for 4 hours. Add water as needed. Brown the remaining onion, bread crumbs, oregano, chili pulp and chili powder in a skillet and add to soup just prior to serving.

Serves 6

Chicken and Corn Soup

Sopa de Pollo y Elote

2 crushed garlic cloves
1/2 onion, diced
1 chopped tomato
Mushrooms
2 tablespoons butter
Chopped coriander, to taste
1 cup cooked and shredded chicken
1 cup chicken stock
1 (8 3/4 ounce) can cream style corn
1 (10 3/4 ounce) can cream of chicken soup
1 can milk
Salt and pepper to taste
(Optional)
2 tablespoons hot sauce

Saute the garlic, onion, tomato and mushrooms in the butter or oil until onions are soft. Add chicken, chicken stock, cream corn, cream of chicken soup, milk and sprinkle coriander. Salt and pepper to taste. Stir lightly and cook over low heat for 12-18 minutes. Add and stir in the hot sauce just before serving .

Serves 4

Chicken Soup

Caldo de Pollo

1 whole chicken
1 onion
2 carrots, peeled and cubed
2 cloves garlic, crushed
2 1/2 stalks celery, cubed
Salt
Pepper
6 cups water

Section the chicken the way you like. In a large pot, bring chicken and all other ingredients to a rolling boil. Then simmer for about 20 minutes. Add salt and pepper. Serve hot with crackers.

Serves 6

Cheese Soup

Caldo de Queso

3/4 pound of new potatoes
5 cups beef broth
2 large tomatoes, uncooked
2 tablespoons oil
1 clove garlic, chopped
1/2 onion, sliced
1 (14 ounce) can of peeled green peppers
1 sprig goosefoot (see glossary)
Strips of mild cheddar cheese
Salt to taste

Peel and dice potatoes. Add the potatoes to the broth after it has been brought to a boil and cool 8-10 minutes. Grate the whole tomatoes and set aside. Fry the onion and garlic in oil until soft. Add the grated tomato and cook for about 10 minutes or until it thickens. Cut peppers into strips and add with goosefoot to the broth. Cook over medium heat for 5-8 minutes. Salt to taste. Add cheese and serve when it has melted.

Serves 6

Lime Soup

Sopa de Limon

12 tortillas cut into strips
1/3 of unpeeled, chopped bitter lime*
4 chicken gizzards
5 chicken livers
9 cloves of garlic, toasted and crushed
3/4 cup chopped onion
1/3 cup chopped serrano peppers
1/4 teaspoon oregano
6 peppercorns
Salt to taste
8 cups water
2 chicken breasts
Pepper
Lard or oil
1/3 cup chopped onion
1/4 cup chopped green peppers
1 large boiled tomato, crushed

Place the chicken gizzards and livers, crushed garlic, oregano, peppercorns, water, pepper, lime, green pepper and 3/4 cup onion in a saucepan and cook for approximately 15 minutes. Salt to taste. Add the chicken breasts and cook for an additional 15 minutes. Strain the broth and keep warm. Chop the liver, remove gristle from gizzards and shred the chicken breasts. Put the meat aside.

Heat the oil and saute 1/3 cup of onion until soft. Add the tomato and cook for 4 to 6 minutes over medium heat. Lower heat and let simmer in covered dish another five minutes. Add the meat and allow to cook. In frying pan, heat oil until very hot and fry the tortilla strips until crisp. Drain on paper towel. Drop the tortilla strips in the broth while still hot and pour broth into soup bowls. Serve the meat dish in another bowl on the side.

*If the bitter lime is not available, use a piece of orange or grapefruit peel with a regular lime.

Serves 6

Mexican Soup

Caldo de Res

1 package of bones with marrow
1 package oxtails
2 pounds of stew meat or meat on round bones
1/2 onion
1/2 bell pepper
2 cloves garlic, crushed
1 sprig coriander
3 potatoes, peeled and cubed
5 carrots, sliced
1/2 cabbage
1/2 celery stalk, cubed
1 tomato, cubed
Salt
Pepper
4 corn on the cob, halved
2 lemons

Packages of bones usually have 3 or 4 to a package. If using pre-packaged corn, don't add until soup is almost done. Boil the bones, corn and meat in about 8 cups water, slowly adding all the other ingredients. Let this mixture boil until the meat has softened. Every now and then skim the foam. Don't overcook. Add salt and pepper. Serve hot with corn tortillas. Squeeze lemon in each serving.

Serves 6-8

Mexican Beef Soup

Caldo

1 pound soup bones
1 clove garlic, crushed
Salt to taste
1/8 teaspoon pepper
5 carrots, cubed
Coriander to taste
1 tomato, cubed
5 potatoes
1/2 head cabbage
5 ears fresh corn
Bell pepper
Celery, diced
Optional:
Oxtails

Boil soup bones and tails in large container of water with pepper, salt, garlic, celery and tomato for 1 hour; add coriander and cook for 1 hour. Add carrots, corn, potatoes and cabbage and cook for 1 hour. Serve with lemon and corn tortillas.

Serves 6-8

Shredded Dry Beef Soup

Caldo de Carne Seca de Res Desmenuzada

1/2 pound of round steak
1/2 tomato
1 onion
3 serrano peppers
1 head of garlic, crushed
Salt and pepper to taste
Pinch of cumin, crushed
1 teaspoon oil

Cut and cube tomato, onion and peppers. This makes a "Pico de Gallo".

Cut the beef in cubes and boil in water until cooked. Reserve water. Take beef out to dry; once it's dry, shred the beef.

Crush head of garlic and cumin. Adding a bit of the water from the beef to this mixture, make a paste. Brush this paste on the meat. In a skillet add the oil and saute *Pico de Gallo*. Add the shredded beef and stir. Add the rest of the water from the beef, add more water if needed. Cover and simmer for 15 minutes. Salt and pepper to taste. Serve with corn tortillas.

Serves 2-4

Tortilla Soup

Sopa de Tortilla

10 corn tortillas, somewhat stale
Salt and pepper to taste
3 garlic cloves, crushed
1/2 onion, cubed
2-3 pasillas peppers
3 tomatoes
2 avocados, cubed (peel and pit)
2 sprigs goosefoot (see glossary)
1 tablespoon oil
Oil for frying
1 small feta cheese, crumbled
1/2 cup thick cream or sour cream
3 limes
6 cups chicken stock
Salt and pepper to taste

Cut tortillas in thin strips. In a small skillet add about 1/2 inch of oil. When hot, add tortilla pieces a few at a time. Fry them all until golden brown. Drain them on a paper towel.

Peel and core the tomatoes; in a blender puree them with garlic and onion. Add 1/4 cup of the stock if needed.

In a skillet use 1 tablespoon of oil, saute tomato puree. Boil for two minutes. Let simmer for 5 minutes or until puree has thickened and changed colors. Stir constantly.

Add remaining chicken stock and goosefoot. Return to a boil adding salt and pepper. Cover and let simmer for 15 minutes.

Remove seeds from peppers and cut them in small rings. Fry in hot oil until crisp. Remove and drain them on a paper towel.

Before serving, reheat soup and add the fried tortilla strips. Garnish each bowl with pepper rings and avocado. Sprinkle each serving with cheese and add a dab of cream in each with a lime.

Serves 4-6

Chili with Meat

Chile con Carne

1 pound ground beef
3 tablespoons chili powder
3 cups water
1 cup onion, chopped
1 (8 ounce) can tomato sauce
Optional:
Jalapenos or picante sauce

Brown meat in skillet. Transfer to large pot. Add tomato sauce, onion, chili powder and water. Bring to boil then reduce heat and simmer at least 30 minutes. For a spicier chili, add jalapenos or picante sauce. If chili with beans is desired, add 1 cup of cooked pinto beans.

Serves 4

Chili with Meat

Jim's Chili con Carne

3 pounds of beef, steak or boneless roast
1 large onion, chopped coarsely
6-10 fresh garlic cloves, crushed
1 large tomato, chopped coarsely
5 ancho peppers, dried
2 cascabel peppers, dried
1 mulato pepper, dried (or medium hot pepper of choice)
1 tablespoon cumin
1/2 teaspoon ground black pepper
Salt to taste
1 tablespoon oil (beef suet can be substituted)

Remove seeds and devein peppers, then place in water and bring to boil, cover until softened. Meanwhile cut meat into medium, stew-sized pieces, set aside. Sprinkle with black pepper. Chop onion coarsely and crush garlic. Put oil or suet fat in large pot, preferably cast iron Dutch oven, on medium heat, and saute onions and garlic. When onions are soft, add meat pieces and brown all sides. Puree pepper pulp in blender with some of the water in which they were boiled. Removing skins is preferable. Add chili puree to meat, blending gradually, and enough chili water to cover. Add cumin and salt. Bring to a boil, cover and lower heat to simmer.

Serves 6-8

Chili with Meat

Tana's Chili con Carne

2 pounds lean ground beef
3 garlic cloves or 3 tablespoons of garlic powder
A pinch of cumin or 1/4 teaspoon of cumin powder
1/4 teaspoon black pepper
3 tablespoons flour
1/4 small onion
1/2 small bell pepper
2 cups water
Salt to taste
3 tablespoons chili powder

If you are using garlic cloves and whole cumin, crush and grind them up.

Brown meat and add onion, bell pepper, salt, pepper, cumin, garlic and flour. Add chili powder and stir. Add your water and bring to a boil. Simmer for about ten minutes.

Use the chili to top enchiladas, hot dogs, beans, corn, chips, burritos or fries.

Yield: 4-6 cups

Mexican Meatball Soup

Meatballs:
1 pound ground beef
1/4 cup masa de harina
1/2 cup hot water
1 egg, beaten
2 tablespoons chopped onion
2 tablespoons picante sauce
1 teaspoon salt
1/2 teaspoon oregano
1/4 teaspoon pepper
Broth:
3 quarts beef stock (canned or homemade)
1 (16 ounce) can tomatoes
1 onion, chopped
4 garlic cloves, crushed
3-4 jalapenos, chopped
3 tablespoons bacon drippings
Optional:
1/2 teaspoon cumin powder

For meatballs: mix all ingredients well and make into balls.
For the broth: fry onions and garlic in bacon drippings. Add tomatoes, beef stock, jalapenos and if desired, 1/2 teaspoon cumin powder. Bring to a boil and drop meatballs into broth. Reduce heat and simmer for 30 minutes. When ready to serve, sprinkle a bit of grated cheese into each bowl. Make yourself some jalapeno cornbread or gorditas and enjoy.

Serves 6-8

Tripe Soup

Menudo

8-10 pounds of tripe
2 large onions
1 whole garlic
1 large package menudo mix
1 small package chili powder
2 pigs feet, cut by butcher in 6 pieces
3 tablespoons salt
Fresh dried oregano
1 tablespoon whole ground cumin
Optional:
1 cow's foot, cut by butcher in 6 pieces

Remove the white fat from tripe and cut up into 3/4 inch to 1 inch pieces. Wash thoroughly and place in very large pot with water to cover. Bring to boil and skim frequently. After all skimming is completed, add the onions (quartered) and the whole garlic pod. Add pigs feet, cows feet, menudo mix and cumin. Cook for at least 3 hours or more, until tripe is soft and pigs feet are tender.

Flavor to taste with additional chili powder and hand crushed oregano.

Serves 18-20

Tripe

Menudo

4 pounds tripe, washed and cut into 1 inch squares
1 large soup bone
2 pig knuckles
8 cloves garlic
2 cups hominy
2 cups onion, chopped
8 or more tablespoons chili powder
4-6 chopped jalapeno peppers
1/2 cup coriander
Salt and pepper to taste

Place tripe, soup bone and pig knuckles in pot with water to cover. Salt to taste. Bring to boil and turn to simmer 6 to 8 hours. Replace water as needed. Skim for fat occasionally. After cooking meat remove any bones. Add other ingredients and cook slowly for another hour. Season to taste. Serve with lime and corn tortillas.

Menudo, like any other soup or stew, always tastes better the next day.

Serves 10

Mexican Stew

Caldillo

3 pounds stew meat
2 onions, chopped
2 tablespoons bacon drippings
4 cups tomatoes, chopped
4 jalapeno peppers, chopped
4 carrots, sliced
1 can beef bouillon
3 garlic cloves
1 tablespoon cumin powder
2 potatoes, cubed
4 short ears of frozen corn on the cob

Saute beef in fat. Add tomatoes, peppers, beef stock and other seasonings. Cook over low heat until meat is tender. Add potatoes, onion, carrots and corn. Cook slowly another 45 minutes or until vegetables are done. Serve with flour tortillas or jalapeno cornbread.

Serves 6

Mexican Stew

Caldillo

1 to 1 1/2 pounds stew meat
1 small onion
1/2 medium bell pepper
1 envelope stew seasoning
3 medium potatoes, cubed
4 carrots, sliced
3 ears corn, cut in 1 inch pieces
1 can mixed vegetables, drained
1 teaspoon hot sauce
1/2 to 1 can tomato sauce
Flour
Water

Brown meat with the chopped onion and bell pepper. Put enough flour to thoroughly coat meat. Add stew seasoning according to instructions on envelope. Add seasoning and enough water to cover meat. Add vegetables, hot sauce and tomato sauce. When vegetables are tender enough, add mixed vegetables. Serve with cornbread.

Serves 4-6

Mexican Pork Stew

Pozole

10 pork chops
4 tablespoons bacon drippings
2 onions, chopped
1 garlic clove, chopped
10-15 sprigs coriander, chopped
2 fresh tomatoes, cubed
2 serrano peppers, sliced
2 teaspoons soy sauce
5 cups water
1 can stewed tomatoes
1 can hominy
Lime
Salt to taste
Pepper
Flour

Cube the pork chops and discard bone and fat. Add salt and pepper and roll in flour. Brown in the bacon grease. Add chopped onions, coriander, sliced peppers, garlic and cubed tomatoes. Add soy sauce and cook for 3 to 5 minutes. Add water and stir. Reduce heat and allow to cook slowly for an hour. Add the canned tomatoes and hominy. Cover and simmer 20 to 30 additional minutes. Squeeze a lime on top before serving.

Serves 6-8

Gazpacho

1 cucumber
1 small onion
1 avocado
1 tomato
1 bell pepper
2 tablespoons salad oil
4 tablespoons wine vinegar
8 cups tomato juice
Juice of 4 limes
3-4 dashes hot sauce
1 teaspoon salt
1/2 pint sour cream
Celery, finely chopped
Croutons and bacon bits for garnish

Finely chop first five ingredients. Mix with next six ingredients. Refrigerate. When thoroughly chilled, serve in cups with sour cream on top of each. Garnish each serving with chopped celery, croutons and bacon bits.

Serves 8

SALADS

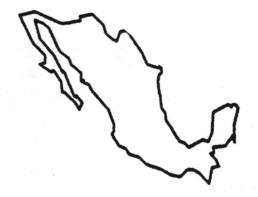

Cactus Salad

Ensalada de Nopalitos

4-6 cacti
1 onion, diced
Olives of choice (for color, use black olives)
3 boiled eggs
Optional:
Bacon bits

Clean, cut and boil cactus for 15 minutes. Let cool. Mix all ingredients. **Suggestion: Cacti can be purchased, ready-to-use, in the special foods sections of produce departments in larger markets.

Serves 2-4

Jicama Salad

Ensalada de Jicama

1 large jicama, peeled and cubed
Mandarin orange, sectioned
Sprinkle of red pepper
1 lemon

Mix all ingredients and chill. Before serving, squeeze lemon juice on salad.

Serves 2

Cucumber Salad

Ensalada de Pepino

4 tablespoons sour cream
3 large cucumbers
4 tablespoons vegetable oil
Pinch of black pepper
Pinch of salt
1 lemon
Pinch of paprika

Peel and slice cucumbers. Rinse in colander and sprinkle salt all over. Let sit for about an hour, allowing the cucumbers to release excess water.

Mix the sour cream, lemon and oil. Don't use any more salt at this point. Mix the cucumbers in the sour cream mixture. Sprinkle with pepper and paprika. Refrigerate and serve.

Serves 4

Avocado Salad

Guacamole

4 ripe avocados
1 tablespoon fresh lemon juice
1/4 cup picante sauce
1/4 cup sour cream or plain yogurt
1 tablespoon grated onion
Crushed garlic to taste
1 jalapeno pepper, minced
1/4 cup coriander, chopped

Scoop out avocado and mash. Add lemon juice to a rough texture. Stir in other ingredients. Serve within one half hour, if possible. Leave 1 or 2 of the avocado seeds in the salad until ready to serve to keep it from turning dark.

Yield: 2 cups

Hot Mexican Beef Salad

Ensalada de Rez

1 pound ground beef
1/4 cup chopped onion
1 (16 ounce) can kidney beans*
1/2 cup french dressing
1/2 cup water
1 tablespoon chili powder
1 large head lettuce, shredded
2 cups sharp cheddar cheese, shredded

Brown meat and drain. Add onions and cook until tender. Stir in beans, dressing, water and chili powder. Simmer for 15 minutes. Stir well and add 1 1/2 cups cheese. Stir again and then top with the remaining cheese. Serve over lettuce.

*Ranch style beans can be substituted for the kidney beans.

Serves 4-6

Stuffed Tomatoes

Jitomates Rellenos

6 firm ripe tomatoes
1 can of tuna, packed in water, drained
1 can of peas
3 spears of celery, cubed
1/2 cup mayonnaise
Salt to taste
Pepper to taste

Place tomatoes in boiling water, only enough to peel them easily.

Mix the tuna, peas, celery, mayonnaise, and seasonings. Cut the tops of the tomatoes and remove some of the pulp. Be careful not to tear them. Fill with the mixture, and serve the tomatoes on a bed of lettuce.

Serves 3

Layered Southwest Salad

Ensalada

Corn tortilla chips*
3 corn tortillas
Vegetable oil
Salad:
1 pound ground beef
1/2 cup chopped onion
1 (7 ounce) can whole kernel corn
1 (6 ounce) can tomato paste
1/2 cup spicy/sweet French dressing
1/2 cup water
1 tablespoon chili powder
1 teaspoon salt
5 cups shredded lettuce
2 tomatoes, chopped
Guacamole: *(see glossary)*
1 cup cheddar cheese, shredded

1) For tortilla chips, cut each tortilla into 6 wedges. Fry tortilla wedges in about 1/2 inch deep hot oil (375 degrees) until lightly browned and crisp; drain on absorbent paper.
2) For salad, brown meat and onion in 10 inch skillet; drain. Combine corn, tomato paste, dressing, water, chili powder and salt. Serve on lettuce and tomatoes. Top with guacamole and cheese.

*If in a hurry, purchased corn chips can be substituted.

Serves 6

Spinach Salad

Ensalada de Espinacas

2 boiled eggs
1 bag of fresh spinach
1/2 of a purple onion, sliced thinly
1 cup plain yogurt
2 teaspoons chopped pecans
2 teaspoons vegetable oil
10 fresh mushrooms
Salt and pepper to taste
1 lemon

Wash spinach, drain thoroughly and tear into small pieces. Rinse and slice mushrooms. Slice the boiled eggs. Add the rest of the ingredients. Chill and serve. Salt and pepper to taste and squeeze on lemon juice.

Serves 4

Taco Salad

1 pound ground beef
1 head of lettuce, shredded
2 chopped tomatoes
1 diced onion
1 cup grated cheddar cheese
1 small can sliced black olives
2 avocados, chopped
1 can ranch style beans, drained*
Corn tortilla chips
1 medium bottle French dressing*

Cook ground beef in water and drain to remove fat. Combine all ingredients in a large salad bowl. Mix well.

*Pinto beans, whole or refried, may be substituted and sour cream instead of dressing can also be used.

Serves 4

Mexican Chef Salad

Ensalada Mexicana

1 pound ground beef
1 onion
1 can (15 ounce) red kidney beans
4 tomatoes
1 head lettuce
1 avocado
4 ounces shredded cheese
1 bag taco-style chips
1 small bottle Thousand Island dressing

Brown meat and add beans; drain well. Simmer together for 10 minutes. Cool. While meat is cooling, shred lettuce in a large bowl. Add chopped onion, cubed tomatoes, cheese and chunked avocado. Add crushed taco chips and then bean and meat mixture. Make ahead of time and serve as a meal or appetizer.

Serves 4-6

EGGS/ BREAKFAST DISHES

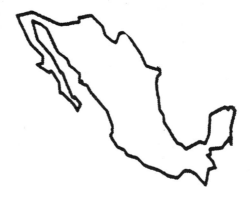

Eggs and Fried Tortilla Squares

Migas

1-2 tortillas cut in 2 inch squares
2 tablespoons oil
2 eggs
Optional:
Picante sauce
Grated cheese
Diced onions
Chopped tomatoes

Place the tortilla squares in oil and fry until golden. Add eggs and scramble until done. Add optional ingredients if desired.

Serves 2

Deluxe Corn Tortillas with Egg

Migas

6 eggs, beaten
1/8 teaspoon salt
1/8 teaspoon black pepper
3/4 cup chopped onion
2 cloves of garlic
2 tablespoons vegetable oil
2 corn tortillas, cut in strips*
1 (4 ounce) can chopped green peppers, drained
1 cup Monterrey Jack cheese, shredded
2 medium tomatoes, peeled and chopped
6 flour tortillas
Picante sauce as desired

Combine eggs, salt and pepper, beat and set aside. Saute onion and garlic in large skillet until tender. Stir in corn tortillas and green peppers. Pour egg mixture into skillet over medium heat, stirring often. Serve with flour tortillas.

*This recipe serves as a way to use somewhat stale corn tortillas in a delicous way.

Serves 4-6

Corn Tortilla Strips with Cheese

Chilaquiles con Queso

6 tortillas
3-4 serrano peppers
2 cloves of garlic
2 large tomatoes
2 cups white or Feta cheese
1/2 onion, chopped
Cooking oil
Salt to taste

Cut tortillas in long strips. In skillet, heat cooking oil until hot. Fry strips of tortillas until they are crispy. Set them in plate with a napkin to soak excess grease.

In a blender or by hand, chop peppers, garlic and tomatoes.

In another skillet, saute chopped onions; add the hot sauce, garlic and tomato mixture and stir. Cut the cheese into strips and add to mixture. Now add the tortilla strips. Let it simmer for 5 minutes.

Serves 3-4

Beans and Eggs

Frijoles con Huevo

2-3 tablespoons oil, bacon or Mexican sausage drippings
1 cup cooked pinto beans
2 eggs, beaten

Heat oil in skillet. Add beans and fry until 1/2 of oil is consumed. Add eggs and scramble until done. Serve with warm tortillas.

Serves 2-3

Tomato and Cheese Surprise

Tomatadas

2 teaspoons cooking oil
1/2 cup white onion
1 cup peeled tomatoes
2 cups white or Feta cheese
5 tortillas

In a skillet saute onions in oil; cut cheese in slices and put into pan. Grate tomatoes into pan. Cut tortillas in quarters and put into pan. Let tortillas soak and soften. Serve with refried beans. Salt to taste.

Serves 3

Sausage and Egg Taquitos

Chorizo con Huevo

1 roll of pork sausage*
6-8 eggs
8 flour tortillas
Salt to taste
Optional:
1/4 cup finely chopped onion
1/4 cup chopped tomato
1 cup cheddar or American cheese, shredded

Brown sausage, and saute; add onion and tomato if desired. Add eggs and salt. Mix egg with sausage until egg is fully cooked. Remove from heat. Fill tortillas with sausage and egg mixture. Top with cheese.

*Refried beans can be substituted for the Mexican sausage to make bean and egg taquitos.

Serves 6-8

Mexican Sausage and Eggs

Chorizo Mexicano con Huevo

1 tablespoon oil
2 links Mexican sausage (about 3/4 cup)
2-3 eggs
Optional:
1/2 onion, chopped
1/2 tomato, chopped

Place sausage in a skillet with oil and cook covered over low to medium heat. Brown, stir for even cooking. Add onions and tomato if desired and saute. Add eggs and scramble until done.

Serves 2

Potato and Mexican Sausage Taquitos

Taquitos de Papas y Chorizo

4 medium potatoes
1 link of Mexican sausage
6 flour tortillas
Shortening or oil
Salt to taste

Peel, wash and dice potatoes. In a skillet or deep fryer, heat shortening and fry potatoes until lightly browned and tender. Drain to remove grease. Add salt to taste. Place potatoes aside in a pan or plate while sausage cooks. Add the potatoes, stir until thoroughly mixed. Remove from heat. Fill tortillas with mixture.

Serves 6-8

Beans and Mexican Sausage

Taquitos de Frijoles y Chorizo

3 cups of refried beans
1 link Mexican sausage
Oil or shortening for frying
4-6 flour tortillas
Salt to taste

Cook sausage on medium until it looks the consistency of browned ground beef; add beans. Salt to taste. Stir until thoroughly mixed together. Heat tortillas and fill with beans and sausage mixture.

Serves 2-3

Eggs Ranchero

Huevos Rancheros

7-8 serrano or jalapeno peppers, fresh
1/2 medium onion
1 medium tomato
2 cloves garlic, crushed
Pinch of cumin, pepper and salt
Olive or cooking oil
2 eggs
1 corn tortilla

Chop peppers and onions coarsely. Chop tomato finely. Heat oil over medium heat and saute onion, peppers and garlic. Add tomato when onions are soft and clear. Continue sauteing until tomato is completely soft; add spices and a little water or tomato juice to make it a little soupy. Lower heat, cover and bring to a fast simmer.

Heat oil in another skillet, dip corn tortilla in hot oil, drain and place on plate. Gently fry eggs. Place on tortilla and smother with sauce. Serve with refried beans.

Serves 1-2

Ranch Style Eggs

Huevos Rancheros (Fritos)

Sauce:
1 large tomato
1/4 onion, chopped
1 clove garlic, crushed
Serrano peppers, to your taste
Eggs:
2 eggs
2 corn tortillas
Vegetable oil to fry
Salt and pepper to taste

Boil and peel tomato; reserve water. In a blender, puree all of the sauce ingredients. Add water from the reserve if needed.

Heat oil in skillet. Pass each tortilla in the oil for a couple of seconds and remove. Fry the eggs. Be careful not to tear them. There should be enough oil in the pan to bathe the egg whites, not the yolk.

On a plate, place tortillas side by side and place an egg on top of each. Add the sauce on top of your dish. Salt and pepper to taste. Serve hot.

Serves 1-2

Tana's Divorced Eggs

Tana's Huevos Divorciados

Red Sauce:
1/2 red tomato
2 red serrano peppers

Boil and put in a blender. Puree.

Green Sauce:
1/2 green tomato
2 jalapenos

Boil and put in a blender. Puree.

4 corn tortillas
4 eggs
Oil
Salt to taste

Heat oil and fry each egg separately, sunnyside up. Heat more oil and pass each tortilla through the oil.

Set 2 tortillas side by side and place an egg on top of each tortilla. Add red sauce to one and green sauce to the other.

Serves 4

Ranch Style Poached Eggs

Huevos Rancheros

1 large white onion
1 green pepper
3 tablespoons olive oil
1/4 cup flour
1 can tomatoes
1 tablespoon salt
1/2 teaspoon chili powder
1 tablespoon chopped parsley
1/2 teaspoon oregano
8 eggs
Sharp cheddar cheese
Ripe olives, pitted

Chop onion and green pepper and saute in oil until tender. Add the flour carefully to prevent the sauce from becoming lumpy. Drain the juice from the tomatoes into the sauce and cook a few minutes. Add tomatoes, herbs and seasoning and cook until the sauce is thick. Place sauce in a buttered casserole and break the eggs, on top of the sauce. Slices of cheese and pitted ripe olives can be placed between the eggs. Place in an oven which has been preheated to 325 degrees until the eggs are covered with a nice film of white. There is enough sauce for 12 eggs. Note: If you refrigerate this sauce, reheat it before placing it in the baking dish.

Serves 4

Cactus and Egg

Nopalitos con Huevo

4-6 tender cacti
1/4 cup diced onion
1 clove garlic, crushed
Salt and pepper to taste
1 large tomato, diced
1 teaspoon fresh coriander, chopped
1 teaspoon oil
2 eggs
Corn tortillas
Optional:
Peppers of choice

Cook cactus by boiling 15 to 20 minutes. Drain. Saute onion and add garlic, pepper or other seasoning to taste. Add tomato and coriander. Simmer 5 minutes. Add eggs and scramble. Serve with warm corn tortillas.

Freshly diced serrano or jalapeno peppers are optional ingredients.

Serves 4-6

Cactus and Eggs

Huevos con Nopales

8 ounce can cactus*
3 tablespoons butter
2 tablespoons heavy cream
6 eggs, lightly beaten
Salt and pepper to taste
Optional:
Picante sauce

Rinse cactus pieces well with cold water and drain thoroughly; heat butter in skillet and saute cactus lightly. Add heavy cream to eggs and season with salt. Scramble eggs into cactus. Season the scrambled egg mixture with freshly ground pepper.

*Fresh cactus that has been cleaned, cut and boiled for 15 minutes may be used instead of canned cactus.

Serves 6

Chocolate Flavored Breakfast Cereal

Champurrado

2 1/2 cups water
1/2 cup flour tortilla mix
1 inch stick of cinnamon
Brown sugar to taste
1 1/2 ounces Mexican chocolate

Bring 1 1/2 cups of water to a boil. Pour the flour tortilla mix into the second cup of water, mix and then strain into the boiling water. Stir frequently. Add the chocolate, cinnamon and brown sugar. Stir for 4 or 5 minutes or until it thickens. Serve warm.

Serves 2-4

TORTILLA
DISHES

Flour Tortillas

2 cups flour tortilla mix*
1/2 cup warm water

Combine flour tortilla mix and water. Two or three more teaspoons of water may be added if necessary. Knead on a lightly floured surface until smooth. Cover and let stand 20 minutes. Shape into 12 small balls. Roll out each ball on lightly floured surface to form a 12 inch circle. Bake on hot 400 degree lightly greased griddle or in a large skillet until browned, about 1 to 2 minutes on each side.

*Flour tortilla mix is a ready-to-use product that may be purchased in your grocery.

Yield: 12 tortillas

Flour Tortillas

2 cups flour
1/4 cup shortening
1 1/2 tablespoons baking powder
1/2 cup warm water
Optional:
1/4 teaspoon salt

Sift the flour and baking powder together. Add the water and form a dough ball. Transfer the dough to a lightly floured board and knead until smooth. Divide dough into 12 small balls and roll out each ball to form a 12 inch circle. Cook on a dry griddle, turning several times until they are done. They will be brown in spots. Use as a bread or with salsas and salads.

It is recommended that the tortilla mix be salted to taste.

Yield: 12 tortillas

Wheat Flour Tortillas

2 cups wheat flour, sifted
1 1/2 tablespoons baking powder
1/2 cup lard or shortening
3/4 cup warm water
1/2 teaspoon salt, or to taste

Knead the lard or shortening into the flour. Put the salt and baking powder into the warm water and stir until dissolved. Knead the water into the dough. Allow to sit for 15 to 20 minutes. Divide into 12-15 balls. Roll out as thin as possible. Cook on griddle for 20-30 seconds on first side and somewhat less on remaining side. Stack and cover.

Yield: 10-12 tortillas

Corn Tortillas

2 cups masa de harina mix*
1 cup water

Combine the *masa de harina* with water and mix well. Add more water (2-3 teaspoons) if necessary to hold dough together. Knead on an unfloured surface to blend well. Separate and shape into 12 small balls. Place each ball of dough between 2 pieces of waxed paper, or plastic wrap, and press out to form a 6 inch circle. It is better to use a rolling pin to flatten the dough. Bake on a hot 400 degree lightly greased griddle or in a large skillet until lightly browned, about 1-2 minutes. Tortillas should be soft and pliable. To make tortilla chips, cut each baked tortilla into 6 wedges and fry in deep hot oil until lightly brown and crisp. For taco shells, place tortilla in 1/2 inch of hot oil, 375 degrees, folding the tortilla with forks or tongs to form a V shell. Fry about 30 seconds per side.

*Masa de harina is a ready-to-use corn mix found in most grocery stores.

Yield: 12 tortillas

Tortillas in Pumpkin Seed Sauce

Tortillas en Salsa de Pepitas

1 (16 ounce) can cooked tomatoes, crushed
2 tablespoons oil
1/4 medium onion chopped
Salt to taste
1 whole habanero pepper
2 large sprigs goosefoot (see glossary)
2 1/2 cups water
1 2/3 cups hulled, toasted pumpkin seeds
5 hard boiled eggs, crumbled and salted
12 corn tortillas
Optional: Pumpkin Seed Oil

Heat the oil in a skillet and saute the onion. Add the tomatoes, salt and whole pepper. Cook over medium heat about 10 minutes or until it thickens. Set aside. Place the goosefoot into the water; add salt and bring to a boil for 3-5 minutes. Place the pumpkin seeds in a shallow dish and sprinkle them with the goosefoot broth. As it cools, knead the seeds until pumpkin seed oil is seen. Tilt the dish and drain the oil into a small container. There should be several tablespoons. Move the pumpkin seed paste to a separate saucepan and stir in remaining broth until smooth. Heat the sauce over very low heat and stir until it thickens. Remove from heat and lightly coat each tortilla. Place some crumbled egg in the tortilla and roll. Line rolled tortillas on dish. Pour any remaining pumpkin seed sauce on the rolled tortillas. Pour the tomato paste made earlier over the tortillas. If desired, decorate with pumpkin seed oil.

Serves 6

Gorditas

2 cups masa de harina mix
1 1/4 cups hot water
1/2 cup lard or shortening

Stir hot water into masa mix little by little until it forms into a ball. Stir in lard until smooth. Form into balls and pat gently forming a circle 3 1/2 inches in diameter. Cook on hot griddle two minutes on one side and slightly less on the other side.

Yield: 10-12 gorditas

Chalupas Deluxe

Chalupas Compuestas

1 cup refried beans
1 cup cooked ground beef*
1 cup shredded cheese, of choice
1 cup mashed avocado, see guacamole recipe
1 cup shredded lettuce
1 cup diced tomato
4 corn tortillas, fried, flat

On each corn tortilla spread beans, then top with ground beef, lettuce, tomato, cheese and avocado.

*Shredded turkey or chicken can be substituted for beef.

Serves 2

Chalupas

2 cups refried beans
8 corn tortillas
1 cup grated cheddar cheese
1 tomato, cubed
1/2 head of lettuce, finely chopped
Hot salsa to taste
Salt
Pepper
1 cup oil to fry

Heat refried beans with a tablespoon of oil. In another skillet, heat oil ready for deep frying. Place tortillas in oil one at a time. They should lay flat and fry until crispy. Set aside on paper towels. Spread refried beans on top of each. Sprinkle with tomato, lettuce, cheese and salsa.

Serves 3-4

Peggy's Chicken Tacos

Tacos de Pollo

---

1 pound boneless chicken, shredded
1 small can of tomatoes
1/2 can green peppers
1 tablespoon chili powder
1/4 cup green bell peppers
1/4 cup onion, chopped
Lettuce, chopped
Tomato, chopped
Salt
Pepper
20 corn tortillas

Saute tomatoes and peppers. Add chili powder, onion and bell peppers. Place tortillas in hot oil and fold in half. Tortillas should be soft. Saute chicken with tomato-chile mixture. Add about 3 tablespoons of mixture in each tortilla. Top with lettuce, tomato and guacamole.

Yield: 15 tacos

Fried Beef Rolls

Flautas Nortenas

1 pound beef stew meat
20 corn tortillas
2 avocados
2 cloves garlic, crushed
2 serrano peppers
Sprigs of coriander
1/2 onion
1 container sour cream
1/4 head of lettuce
1 tomato
1 box of toothpicks
Salt to taste
4 tablespoons cooking oil

Simmer meat until cooked. Take meat out and let dry. Once the meat is dry, shred. Fill each corn tortilla with shredded beef and pin with toothpick. Fry until golden brown.

Crush the garlic and peppers in a separate bowl; peel and remove seed from avocados and mash. To this mixture add the crushed garlic, peppers, coriander and cubed onion. This makes a guacamole mix. Serve *flautas* with the guacamole and sour cream on a bed of lettuce and tomatoes.

Serves 10-12

Tortilla Chips

Totopos

6 corn tortillas
Melted lard or vegetable oil (1/4 inch deep)

Cut tortillas into triangles (dip or mini size). Heat the lard
or oil; once it is very hot, gently place the tortillas with
prongs into the oil. Brown them evenly and drain on paper
towels. These can be used for all sorts of dips.

Yield: 24-30 chips

Tamales

Tamale filling:
3 pounds chopped beef, pork or chicken
1 large onion
2-4 cloves garlic, mashed
2 1/2 tablespoons chili mix
Salt and pepper to taste
2 tablespoons bacon drippings or shortening

Masa dough:
1 cup shortening
2 1/2 cups masa de harina
2 teaspoons chili powder
1 teaspoon salt
1 3/4 cups water
Corn shucks for wrapping

Heat shortening. Saute onion and garlic for 2 minutes; add meat and brown. Drain off any excess fat. Add remaining ingredients. Simmer covered for 20 minutes.

Masa **dough:** Beat shortening until fluffy. Add *masa*, chili powder, salt and water; beat until light and fluffy or until a spoonful floats in warm water.

To assemble: Soak corn shucks for 1 hour in warm water until soft and pliable; remove silk and keep in pan of water until ready to spread *masa*. Spread shuck with 1 tablespoon of *masa*, at one side, to make about a 4 inch wide strip, add a tablespoon of the meat mixture across the middle of the strip (to look like a cigar). Roll up, as for a jelly roll, starting with the side of the dough even with the edge of the shuck. Fold one end up tightly. Stack *tamales* open end up into a colander or cake rack. Steam by placing colander in a large vessel of steaming water brought to a gentle boil. Do not let water touch any part of the *tamale* during steaming. Test for doneness after one hour. If *masa* leaves the shuck, *tamale* is done.

Yield: 2 dozen

Sweet Tamales

Dry corn husks
4 1/2 cups masa de harina mix
2 2/3 cups warm water
1 1/2 cups lard
3/4 cup sugar
1 teaspoon salt
1/2 teaspoon ground cinnamon
1 cup raisins
1 cup chopped mixed candied fruits and peels
1/4 cup chopped pine nuts or almonds

Soak corn husks in warm water several hours or overnight to soften. Pat dry with paper towels before using. Overlap corn husks, if necessary, to make twelve 8x6 inch pieces. In bowl, mix together *masa de harina* and warm water. Cover and let stand 20 minutes. In large mixer bowl beat togther lard, sugar, salt and cinnamon until fluffy. Beat lard mixture into the *masa* mixture until well combined. Combine raisins, fruits, peels and pine nuts. Measure 1/4 cup of the masa dough 5 inches down long side of wrapper to within 1 1/2 inches of ends. Spread dough upward from edge 4 inches. One inch from edge of dough spoon 2 tablespoons of filling in a row across tamale. Roll tamale, jelly roll style, starting at edge nearest filling. Tie wrapper ends tightly with string or a strip of corn husk. Place tamales in a single layer on a rack in a large steamer or electric skillet. Add water just below the level of the rack. Bring to a boil. Cover and steam over medium heat 45 minutes to an hour until husk peels easily away from tamale, adding boiling water as necessary. Unwrap carefully. Serve warm.

Yield: 12 tamales

Panuchos

8 gorditas (see recipe)
2 cups pinto beans, cooked and mashed
10 tablespoons oil
1 1/2 cups tomatoes, crushed
2 cups chicken, cooked and shredded
Cumin
Garlic
Pepper
Salt

Split the *gordita* to make a "pocket" on one side. Put the mashed beans in the pocket and fry the stuffed tortillas in the oil. Remove and drain on a paper towel. In a separate pan, fry the crushed tomatoes in 4 tablespoons oil. Add chicken, cumin, garlic, pepper and salt. Bring mixture to a boil and serve on top of the fried tortillas.

Serves 4

Nori's Burritos

3 links of Mexican sausage or Tana's chili (see recipe)
1 pound cooked beans
Dough for flour tortillas (see recipe)
2 cups oil for frying
Optional:
Lettuce
Tomato
Cheese of choice

In a skillet, saute sausage or heat Tana's chili. Mash in beans and cook to consistency of refried beans. Set aside to cool. Roll out dough as for tortillas. Fill tortillas with 1/4 cup of filling. Close and fold in both ends, then roll tortillas. Fry until golden on all sides. For burrito deluxe, shred lettuce and cheese. Place burrito on bed of lettuce, top with cheese.

Serves 10

Tortilla Cheese Snacks

Quesadillas

2 cups masa de harina
2 tablespoons all purpose flour
1/2 teaspoon baking powder
1/2 teaspoon salt
2 tablespoons melted butter
1 egg
1/2 cup milk
1 cup shredded cheese of choice

Mix the dry ingredients thoroughly. Add the melted butter, egg and enough milk to form a fairly stiff dough. Form into tortillas and use for *quesadillas*. Fill with cheese and fold in half. On a hot griddle, toast the *quesadillas* until the cheese melts.

Serves 8-10

Mexican Cornbread

Pan de Maiz

1 cup flour
1-2 tablespoons sugar
1/2 tablespoon salt
1 tablespoon baking powder
1 cup cornmeal
2 eggs, beaten
1 cup milk
3 tablespoons oil
3 slices of bacon, crumbled
2 chopped jalapeno peppers, canned or fresh
1/4 small onion, chopped

Preheat oven to 375 degrees. Sift flour, sugar, salt and baking powder. Stir cornmeal into flour mixture. Combine beaten eggs, milk and oil. Add to dry ingredient mixture. Saute bacon with jalapenos and onion. Add to batter and mix together until bacon mixture looks evenly distributed. Bake in 8x8x2 pan for about 40 minutes or until toothpick in center comes out clean.

Serves 4-6

Jalapeno Cornbread

Pan de Maiz con Jalapeno

1 cup cream style corn
1 teaspoon sugar
2 teaspoons salt
3 cups yellow cornmeal
1 1/2 teaspoons baking powder
1 cup chopped onion
1 1/3 cup grated cheese
1 cup vegetable oil
3 eggs
1 3/4 cups sweet milk
1/2 cup chopped jalapeno peppers

Preheat oven to 350 degrees. Mix cornmeal, sugar, salt and baking powder together. Combine oil, eggs and milk. Add to dry mixture. Mix in cream corn, onion, grated cheese and peppers. Stir and mix well. Pour into a 9x16 ungreased pan and bake for one hour.

Serves 10

Mexican Casserole

1 dozen corn tortillas cut into 1 inch strips
2 (6 ounce) cans tomato soup
1 can water
Salt
Pepper
1 garlic clove, crushed
2 packages sliced American cheese
Paprika
1 chopped onion
1 (8 ounce) can green peppers, roasted and peeled
2 pounds ground meat
1 tablespoons chili powder

Heat tomato soup and water. Brown and season meat with salt, pepper and garlic. Alternate the following ingredients in casserole; meat, peppers, onion, cheese and strips of tortillas. Pour soup over top and sprinkle with paprika. Cook at 300 degrees for 20 minutes.

Serves 6-8

Beef Crepes

Chimichangas

Flour tortillas
1 pound ground beef
1 small onion, chopped
1 teaspoon garlic powder
Pinch of cumin
1/2 pound of jack or cheddar cheese
Oil for frying
Optional:
1 teaspoon oregano leaves
Taco sauce or hot sauce

Brown meat in skillet with onion and spices. In the center of each tortilla place 1/4 cup of meat and sprinkle with cheese. Roll tortillas, folding ends over and securing with a toothpick. Brown the stuffed tortilla in hot oil, or place on cookie sheet. Bake in a 350 degree oven for 20 minutes. Serve with sauce of choice.

Serves 4-6

Chicken Tortilla Crepes

Chimichangas de Pollo

1 (3 pound) chicken, boiled
2 (10 3/4 ounce) cans cream of chicken soup
1 (4 ounce) can green peppers, diced
1 pound cheddar or Monterrey Jack cheese
1 pint sour cream
1 (4 ounce) can sliced ripe olives
12 flour tortillas

Debone chicken and shred. Mix sour cream, soup, olives, green peppers and half of cheese. Divide soup mixture in half. To one half, add chicken. Spoon chicken mixture onto 12 tortillas and roll. Place in greased ovenproof baking dish. Cover with remaining soup mixture. Top with remaining cheese. Bake at 350 degrees for 20 to 30 minutes, until bubbly. This is good to prepare ahead and freezes well. Delicious at brunch with fresh fruit salad and muffins. At dinner, serve with green salad and popovers.

Serves 8-10

Karen's Mexican Chicken Casserole

1 (14 ounce) can tomatoes*
1 can cream of chicken soup
1/2 medium onion
1 teaspoon pepper
1/8 teaspoon chili powder
1/2 teaspoon salt
8 corn tortillas
2 cups chicken, cooked, boned and diced
10 ounces cheddar cheese, grated

Using a blender, combine tomatoes, soup, onion and seasoning until liquid. In a mixing bowl, combine 1/2 of the liquid mixture with the chicken. Dip the tortillas in the remaining liquid. Coat inside of a 2 quart casserole dish with a nonstick spray. Line bottom of dish with tortillas, pour layer of chicken mixture over them; then another layer of tortillas, etc., ending with chicken mixture. Top with the grated cheese. Bake at 350 degrees for 20 to 30 minutes or until bubbly.

*Fresh, boiled tomatoes could be substituted.

Serves 5

Chicken Enchilada Casserole

4 pounds of chicken
1 large onion, diced
2 garlic cloves, crushed
2 small cans chopped green peppers
1 can cream of mushroom soup
1 can cream of chicken soup
2 dozen tortillas
1 pound cheddar cheese, grated
Oil to fry

Boil chicken until tender, remove from broth to cool. Reserve 2 cups of broth. Debone chicken and shred. Saute onion. Add broth, salt, pepper, garlic and chopped chicken. To this mixture add peppers and soups and heat thoroughly. Cut tortillas into quarters. In a 4 to 6 quart dish, arrange layers of tortillas, chicken mixture and cheese, ending with cheese. Cover and bake at 350 degrees for 35 minutes or until bubbly.

Serves 8-10

Chilaquiles Casserole Style

4 tablespoons cooking oil
1 diced onion
1 bell pepper, chopped
1 (14 ounce) can tomatoes
1 (14 ounce) can tomatoes with peppers
1 (6 ounce) can green peppers (mild)
1 (4 ounce) can tomato sauce
1 cup cooking oil
20 corn tortillas
2 cups grated cheddar cheese
1 cup sour cream

In a large skillet, saute onions and bell pepper in cooking oil. Next add canned peppers, tomato sauce and tomatoes; let simmer for 15 minutes. Cut tortillas in quarters and dip in hot cooking oil. In a buttered casserole dish place a layer of tortillas, cover with tomato sauce, and sprinkle grated cheese. Continue the layers until casserole dish is nearly filled. Spread sour cream over last layer. Bake at 350 degrees for 30 minutes.

Serves 5-6

Meatless Tamale Pie

Tamales de Masa

1 cup yellow cornmeal
2 cups milk
1 large onion, finely chopped
1/2 green pepper, chopped
1/2 cup salad oil
3 1/2 cups tomatoes
3 eggs slightly beaten
1 can whole kernel corn
2 cups ripe olives, pitted
1 tablespoon salt
1/2 cup grated cheese

Cook cornmeal and milk as per instructions for mush. Lightly brown onion and pepper in oil. Add tomatoes and seasonings and simmer for about 20 minutes. Mix eggs with mush, tomatoes, corn and olives. Put in a greased casserole dish. Top with 1/2 cup grated cheese. Bake at 350 degrees for 1 hour or until firm.

*1 1/2 pounds lean ground beef or pork can be browned and shredded if meat is desired.

Serves 8

Tillie's Enchiladas

1/4 cup oil
1 1/2 cups onion, chopped
1 1/2 tablespoons garlic salt
1 teaspoon chili powder
1 teaspoon chili mix
3 tablespoons flour
2 cups water
4 1/2 cups grated cheddar cheese
2 cups onion, chopped
1 dozen corn tortillas

Saute onions in oil. Add garlic salt, chili powder and chili mix. Stir in flour and 2 cups water to make a smooth sauce. Add 1 1/2 cups grated cheese and stir. Combine remaining cheese and 2 cups onion to make filling. Warm up tortillas to soften. Dip tortillas into sauce. Add cheese-onion filling and roll up. Place side by side in baking dish and pour remaining filling on top. Heat at 375 degrees for 15 minutes.

Serves 4-6

Crab Meat Enchiladas

Jaibaladas

1/4 cup butter
1 onion, diced
1 green pepper, diced
1 teaspoon salt
1 teaspoon pepper
2 cups dried crab meat (1 pound)
1/2 cup water
2 medium tomatoes, diced
1 teaspoon chili powder
1/2 teaspoon cumin
1 cup cooking oil
25 corn tortillas
16 ounces grated Swiss cheese

In a large skillet melt the butter and add the onions, green pepper, salt and pepper. Saute until onions are soft and add the crab meat. Heat for five minutes, stirring occasionally. Then add the water, tomatoes, chili powder and cumin. Simmer for 10 minutes. In another skillet, heat the oil and quickly dip the tortillas for a few seconds. Fill the tortillas with drained meat sauce and cheese and roll up. Place side by side in a pan and cover with remaining meat sauce. Add the remaining cheese and bake in a 350 degree oven until cheese is melted and hot, or about 15 minutes.

Serves 5-6

Border Brand Enchiladas

2 pounds ground chuck
1/2 cup onion
1 teaspoon garlic salt
1/2 teaspoon salt
1/2 teaspoon seasoned pepper
1/2 cup tomatoes
1 ounce chili mix
1 (15 ounce) can enchilada sauce
1 (8 ounce) can tomato sauce
1/2 cup sharp cheese, grated
1 1/2 cups American cheese, grated
20 corn tortillas

In sauce pan, saute ground chuck, onions, garlic salt, salt and seasoned pepper for 20 minutes. Add tomatoes and chili mix; simmer for 20 minutes.

Heat enchilada and tomato sauces. Mix cheeses together. On a warm tortilla, put 2 tablespoons of meat mixture and sprinkle with cheese. Roll up and place in a casserole dish. Pour remaining sauce over enchiladas, then add remaining meat. Top with cheese. Bake at 350 degrees for 15 minutes or until heated through.

Serves 6

Chicken Enchiladas

Enchiladas de Pollo

1 pound boiled tomatoes
1 clove garlic
2 toasted serrano peppers
2 tablespoons oil
Salt to taste
1/2 cup sour cream
1 1/2 cups chicken, cooked and shredded
12 corn tortillas
1 onion, chopped
1 cup grated longhorn cheese
1 cup oil for frying

Place the tomatoes, garlic and serrano peppers in a blender and blend until smooth. Fry this sauce in oil for 4-6 minutes until it thickens. Salt to taste and allow to cool for a few minutes. After cooling, stir in sour cream over low heat without bringing to a boil. In a frying pan, heat oil and fry the tortillas for a few seconds on each side without allowing them to become crisp. Stack on paper towels. Dip the tortillas one at a time in the sauce. Place the shredded chicken and chopped onion on each and roll. Place in a greased baking dish. Sprinkle with remaining chopped onion and cheese. Bake at 350 degrees for eight to ten minutes and serve immediately.

Serves 6

Classic Meatless Enchiladas

Enchiladas sin Carne

1 mulato pepper
6 ancho peppers, dried
Fresh corn tortillas
1/2 cup oil
1 large onion, minced or very finely chopped
1 pound Mexican, white or feta cheese*
2 garlic cloves, crushed
1 teaspoon cumin
Salt
Pepper
1 cup chicken broth

Place dried peppers in sauce pot, cover with water and boil gently. Heat most of the oil in small skillet over medium heat. In larger skillet heat 1 teaspoon oil on low heat. Mince onion and place inor bowl. Crumble or grate cheese in another bowl. Bring out serving dish.

When peppers are softened, remove pulp from skins and chop finely or puree in blender. Add this to larger skillet with crushed garlic, raise heat somewhat and saute, stirring constantly. As mixture thickens, gradually add chicken broth, cumin, pinches of salt and pepper. Continue cooking over medium heat until you have a rich, dark, almost syrupy sauce, then lower to simmer.

If working from left to right, place tortillas to left of hot oil skillet and with tongs quickly dip one in hot oil, then drop tortilla in simmering sauce until well coated on both sides; bring out to platter or serving dish. Place on dish, put in large pinch of minced onions and larger pinch of crumbled cheese, then roll up. Repeat with each tortilla. When all tortillas are rolled, sprinkle remaining cheese. Serve immediately or place in oven for a few minutes before serving.

Note: It is important that the tortillas remain soft at all times and that the sauce is the main flavor that you taste, but only in combination with the onion and the sharp, fresh cheese. Do not overcook.

*If Mexican cheese is not available, substitute with cheese of choice.

Serves 6-8

Green Enchiladas

Enchiladas Verdes

1 chicken (2 1/2 to 3 pounds)
2 teaspoons salt
1 small onion
1 clove garlic
1/2 cup tomato, chopped
2 tablespoons onion, chopped
Green sauce (see recipe)
Corn tortillas
1/2 cup oil

Cover chicken with water, add salt, onion and garlic. Cover and cook until very tender. Remove bones from chicken and chop meat up finely. Season with salt and pepper, add chopped onion and tomato and fry mixture lightly for a few minutes in one tablespoon shortening. Pass tortillas in hot oil until soft. Stuff each tortilla with mixture. Place in a baking dish, seam side down. Top with green sauce and bake for 10 minutes.

Serves 4-6

Shrimp Enchiladas Ole

1 cup boiled popcorn shrimp
1/2 cup cooked spinach (fresh or canned)
1/2 cup grated Swiss cheese
1/2 cup grated mozzerella cheese
6 flour or corn tortillas
1 can cream of mushroom soup
3 ounces soft cream cheese
Salt and pepper to taste
Oil to fry

Mix shrimp, spinach and Swiss cheese. In a skillet fill 1/4 inch with oil. Oil must be hot. Pass each tortilla through oil for a few seconds and set aside on a paper towel to soak up excess oil. Fill each tortilla with shrimp mixture and roll. Place in dish. Blend cream cheese and mushroom soup in a blender. Warm up soup and pour over enchiladas. Sprinkle with mozzarella cheese. Heat until cheese melts. Season to taste.

Serves 2-3

Spanish Casserole

1 pound ground chuck
6 tortillas
6 ounces of olives, chopped or sliced
2 cups cheese, grated
1 onion, chopped
1 (10 ounce) can enchilada sauce
1 can cream of chicken soup

Saute beef and onion until brown. Tear each tortilla into strips. Combine all ingredients, except cheese, mixing well. In a 1 1/2 quart ovenproof casserole dish, place half of meat mixture and top with half of cheese. Repeat meat and cheese layers. Cover casserole and bake at 350 degrees for 45 minutes. Uncover and continue to bake a few minutes longer.

Serves 4-6

Taco Casserole

1 pound ground beef
1 medium onion, chopped
8 ounces tomato sauce
1/4 cup water
1 teaspoon chili powder
16 ounces refried beans
1/4 cup taco sauce
1 1/2 cups shredded Monterrey Jack
3 cups tortilla chips, crushed
1 cup lettuce, shredded
1 small tomato, chopped
1/4 cup green onion, sliced
1/4 cup sliced ripe olives, pitted
1/4 cup avocado

Brown beef in skillet or microwave. Add onion and cook until tender. Drain, then stir in tomato sauce, water and chili powder; simmer until bubbly. Meanwhile, stir together beans and taco sauce. Spread in bottom of a 12x7&1/2x2 inch baking dish, then spread the meat mixture on top. Heat through in microwave or oven. Top with cheese and crushed tortilla chips and lettuce. Garnish with tomato, green onion, olives and avocado dip.

Serves 6

Enchilada Casserole

3 1/2 cups chili, (see recipe)
1 1/2 pounds American cheese
20 corn tortillas
Oil or shortening
Optional:
Onion

Grate cheese and chop onion. In a skillet, heat oil just hot enough to soften corn tortillas. In a dish, place a layer of softened tortillas and spread alternating layers of chili, cheese, and tortillas until casserole dish is filled. Finish with a top layer of cheese. Heat in microwave or oven until bubbling. Serve alone or with rice or beans.

Serves 6

Mexican Casserole

20 small corn tortillas
2 cups chicken, shredded
1 cup sour cream
1/2 pound cheese, grated
2 cups tomatillos, (see glossary)
2 garlic cloves, crushed
1/4 teaspoon sugar
1/2 cup water
7-8 poblano peppers
1/3 onion, sliced
3 teaspoons oil
1/3 cup oil
Salt to taste

Place the *tomatillos*, garlic, sugar, water and salt into a blender and blend until sauce is smooth. Cook on medium heat until it thickens. Remove the seeds and devein the peppers, then cut into strips. Heat the oil and saute onions until soft. Add the peppers and salt. Cook 8-10 minutes. Heat the corn tortillas in oil for a few seconds on each side. Stack on paper towels. Bake in three layers. Place 1/3 of the tortillas on the bottom of a greased baking dish. Cover with half the chicken and peppers and 1/3 of the sauce, sour cream and cheese. Repeat. Bake 25-30 minutes in a preheated oven at 350 degrees.

*Shredded pork can be used instead of chicken.

Serves 6

PASTA AND RICE

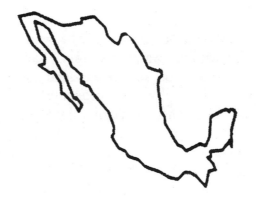

Mexican Rice

Arroz a la Mexicana

1 1/4 cups long grain rice
4 tablespoons oil
8 ounces peeled, seeded and pureed tomatoes
1 tablespoon minced onion
1 cup water
1/2 teaspoon salt
1 (8 ounce) can green peas
2 cups hot chicken broth
2 links Mexican sausage
1 teaspoon minced parsley

The rice should be soaked in hot water for 15 minutes. Rinse rice with tap water and drain. Saute rice in oil while stirring. Add onion and tomato and cook over high heat until rice is almost dry. Stir frequently. Add the water, salt and peas. Lower heat to simmer uncovered until almost dry again. Add broth and cover. Cook on low heat until rice separates easily. As the rice is cooking, take the sausage from its wrapping and fry in a skillet until brown. Empty cooked rice on platter and crumble sausage and parsley on top.

Serves 4

Rice

Arroz

1 cup long grain rice
3 tablespoons cooking oil
1 onion, diced
1 garlic clove, diced
1 1/2 teaspoons salt
1/4 teaspoon chili powder
3 ounce can tomato sauce
2 1/4 cups water

In a large skillet, brown the rice in the oil. Add the remaining ingredients. Let simmer, covered, over low heat for 25 minutes or until tender.

Serves 4-6

Erika's Famous Mexican Rice

Arroz a la Mexicana

2 cups long grain rice
2 tablespoons onion, chopped
2 tablespoons red bell pepper, chopped
2 tablespoons green bell pepper, chopped
2 cups water
4 ounces tomatoes, peeled and boiled
1 garlic clove, crushed
Pinch of cumin, crushed
1/4 cup tomato sauce
1 1/2 cubes chicken bouillon
Salt
Pepper
Oil to fry

In a skillet, saute rice, onion, red and green bell peppers until rice is brown. Add water, tomatoes, garlic, cumin, tomato sauce and chicken bouillon. Cover and cook for 25-30 minutes. Season to taste.

Serves 6-8

Black Rice

Arroz Negro

2 cups long grain rice
4 tablespoons oil
1 medium onion, minced
4 garlic cloves, minced
4 cups hot bean broth (see pinto bean recipe)
Salt to taste
Optional:
Stew Meat
Vegetable of Choice

Soak the rice in hot water for about 15 minutes. Rinse in cold water and drain. Heat oil in skillet and add rice with onion and garlic. Stir and cook until the rice is opaque. Drain oil. Add hot bean broth and salt. Bring to a boil*, then lower heat and allow to simmer for 25-30 minutes.

*Before bringing the rice to a boil, any vegetable or meat can be added to improve the flavor.

Serves 6

Chicken with Rice

Arroz con Pollo

1/2 chicken, cooked and cubed (reserve 2 cups of stock)
1 cup long grain rice
1/4 sliced bell pepper
1 ounce tomato sauce*
1 tablespoon oil
Dash of cumin
2 garlic cloves, crushed

Fry rice in oil over medium heat with bell pepper slices, cumin and garlic until golden brown, stirring to prevent sticking. Add pieces of boiled chicken and tomato sauce to rice. Add 2 cups of chicken stock to the rice mixture. Allow to cook for 25-30 minutes on medium heat. Add hot water as necessary.

*Instead of tomato sauce, 1 small diced tomato may be used.

Serves 4-6

Tana's Vermicelli

Tana's Fideo

5 ounces dry vermicelli*
1/2 pound stew or ground beef
1/4 teaspoon cumin powder or pinch of whole crushed cumin
1/4 teaspoon black pepper
1/4 teaspoon garlic powder or 2 garlic cloves, crushed
1/4 onion, chopped
1/4 bell pepper, chopped
Salt to taste
3 cups water

Brown meat with onion and bell pepper. Add cumin, pepper, garlic and salt. In a separate pan, brown the vermicelli. Add hot water and ingredients from other pan and bring all ingredients to a boil. Simmer 20-30 minutes.

*For variety, use pasta shells or macaroni instead of vermicelli.

Serves 4

Vermicelli Soup

Sopa de Fideo

2 cups vermicelli
1 tomato, cubed
1/4 onion, cubed
Pinch of cumin, crushed
1 sprig of parsley
1 serrano pepper
Oil to fry
1 chicken bouillon cube
Salt to taste
1 garlic clove, crushed
Optional:
1 pound ground beef or 1 pound steak, cubed

In a skillet add oil and brown vermicelli. Add garlic, cumin, onion and tomato. Stir rapidly, not letting the vermicelli stick to pan. Add the bouillon and about 8 cups of water. Let it boil. Add peppers and parsley and simmer until the vermicelli has softened. Add salt to taste. While vermicelli is browning, brown meat in a separate skillet. Add to vermicelli and simmer.

Serves 4-6

Spaghetti with Clams

Espagueti Marinera

2 pounds of clams in shells*
1/4 chopped onion
2 tomatoes, cubed
Oil
1/2 can tomato sauce
Salt
Pepper
1 small package of spaghetti or 5 ounces dry vermicelli

Scrub and wash the clams. Boil them in water until they crack open (about 8-10 minutes). Discard any clams that do not open. Remove the meat and save the water. In a skillet saute onions and tomatoes. Add some of the water from the clams and tomato sauce and simmer. In a large pot, boil the spaghetti with one teaspoon of oil added to water. Boil until cooked and drain. Mix the spaghetti and sauce. Serve hot with garlic bread. Salt to taste.

*2 cans chopped clams may be substituted for fresh clams.

Serves 4-6

Margaret's Mexican Spaghetti

Fideo

1 1/2 large onions, chopped
2 bell peppers, chopped
4 garlic cloves, crushed
2 pounds ground chuck
5 tablespoons chili powder
1 1/2 teaspoons cumin
1 1/2 teaspoons oregano
4 ounces tomato sauce
3-4 cups water
12 ounces spaghetti
1 tablespoon salt
1 cup sharp cheese, grated

Saute onion, bell pepper and garlic. Add meat and brown.
Add chili powder, cumin, spaghetti and salt to taste. Add
water and cook for 20 minutes or until spaghetti is cooked.
Pour in large pan and top with grated sharp cheese. Bake
until cheese melts.

Serves 10-12

BEANS

Chili Beans

Frijoles y Chili con Carne

2 pounds ground round or chuck
1/2 large onion, chopped
1 garlic clove, crushed
Pinch of cumin
Pinch of oregano
2 tablespoons chili powder
1/2 cup tomato sauce
Salt to taste
2 cups hot water
2 medium tomatoes, diced
1 pound cooked pinto beans

In a large pot place meat, onion, garlic and cumin. Cook until lightly browned. Add oregano, tomatoes, chili powder, tomato sauce, beans, salt and water. Bring to boil, lower heat. Simmer for 1 hour. Skim off fat during cooking.

Serves 6-8

Pinto Beans

Frijoles

2 cups pinto, black or red kidney beans
2 onions, finely chopped
2 garlic cloves, chopped
Sprig of goosefoot* or 1 bay leaf
2 serrano peppers, chopped or 1 teaspoon dried pequin
Peppers
3 tablespoons lard
Salt and pepper to taste
1 tomato peeled, seeded and chopped

Wash beans and soak 1-2 hours. Boil beans, onion, garlic, goosefoot or bay leaf and peppers. Cover and simmer gently, adding more water, always hot, as needed. When beans begin to wrinkle add one tablespoon lard or oil. After 2 hours or when beans are tender, add seasoning. Cook another half hour without adding more water; they should not be too watery. Add the remaining chopped onion and garlic and cook until tender. Add tomato and cook for 1-2 minutes.

*see glossary

Serves 6-8

Pinto Beans

Frijoles

1/2 pound pinto beans
5 cups boiling water
1 tablespoon vegetable oil or shortening
1 teaspoon salt
Optional:
Pork rinds or bacon*

Wash 1/2 pound beans; add beans to 5 cups boiling water, boil 3 minutes, cover and let stand 1 hour. Rinse and drain thoroughly. In large pot, place soaked beans, 3 cups of hot water, vegetable oil or shortening and salt. Boil gently with lid ajar 20-25 minutes or until beans are tender.

Note: Beans are more digestible when soaked for a longer period of time. Tip: Leftover beans can be packaged in freezer-proof containers and frozen.

*For extra flavor, add bacon or raw pork rinds while boiling.

Yield: 3 cups

Refried Beans

Frijoles Refritos

1/2 pound cooked pinto beans
3 tablespoons shortening, oil or bacon drippings
Black pepper

In a skillet, heat shortening and add beans. Mash until beans are creamy and beginning to dry. Add pepper to taste. If thickness is needed, add touch of flour. If too dry, add shortening. Serve with any main dish.

Yield: 2 cups

Tana's Beans

Tana's Frijoles

2 pounds pinto beans
1/2 cup shortening or lard
1 garlic clove, crushed
1/4 small onion
Salt

To clean, take all the rocks and broken pieces out of beans. Soak beans in hot water for about an hour. Rinse and put beans in large pot of water. Add all other ingredients. The beans will need water, but it is important to add only hot water. Cook for three hours or until tender on medium heat. Salt to taste.

Serves 10

Beans Ole

Frijoles a la Charra

2 pounds pinto beans
1/2 cup shortening or lard
1 garlic clove, crushed
1/2 small onion, cubed
1/2 tomato, cubed
8 sprigs of coriander
Water to boil
Salt to taste

Clean beans by taking out all the rocks and broken pieces. Soak beans for an hour. Rinse and cook beans in a large pot of water. Add lard and vegetables. Add water as needed to keep beans covered; remember to add only hot water. This will be easier if you have a small pot of water on low heat while the beans are cooking. Cook for three hours or until tender on medium heat.

In a separate skillet, saute garlic, onion, tomato and coriander. If you are having company and are not sure that everyone likes *frijoles a la charra*, then add 2-3 cups of beans to the saute mixture.

Serves 6-8

MEATS

Nina's Special Chicken

1/4 cup flour
3 pounds chicken pieces
5 tablespoons olive oil
1 cup green pepper, diced
1/2 cup onion, chopped
1 garlic clove, minced
1/2 pound mushrooms
1 (14 1/2 ounce) can tomatoes, chopped
1/2 cup water
5 tablespoons Italian herb seasoning
1 teaspoon salt
3 tablespoons red pepper
1/2 cup long grain rice, uncooked

Dredge chicken in flour and shake off excess. Heat oil in a large heavy Dutch oven. Add chicken, a few pieces at a time and brown. Remove chicken to a separate bowl. Add green pepper, onion, garlic and oil to pan and saute 5 minutes. Add mushrooms and saute 3 minutes. Stir in tomatoes, water, Italian seasoning, salt and pepper. Bring to a boil and stir in rice. Return chicken to pan. Cover and cook over low heat for 30 minutes or until chicken is tender and all liquid is absorbed.

Serves 4-6

Chicken with Rice

Arroz con Pollo

2 tablespoons oil
1 cup long grain rice
1/2 medium onion, diced
1/4 teaspoon whole black pepper
1 garlic clove, crushed
2 chicken breasts
3 cups water or chicken broth
1 can tomato sauce
1/2 teaspoon salt
Optional:
Bell pepper

Fry rice in shortening until brown. Add onion, black pepper and garlic. Then add the chicken, water, tomato sauce, bell pepper, and salt. Cover and simmer for 25 minutes. Stir before serving.

Serves 6

Chicken in Mole Sauce

Pollo en Mole

Oil for browning
2 (3 pound) chicken fryers, sectioned
1/4 cup sesame seeds
1 cup almonds, sliced
1/3 cup pumpkin seeds, shelled
1 cup crushed corn tortilla chips
1 cup onion, diced
2 teaspoons garlic, finely minced
1 (16 ounce) can tomatoes
2 cups chicken broth
2 tablespoons lime juice
1 teaspoon ground cinnamon
2 tablespoons cocoa
2-4 serrano peppers, finely minced
Salt and pepper to taste

Heat 3 tablespoons oil in large skillet. Brown chicken.. Add more oil to pan when necessary. Place chicken in a single layer in a large shallow casserole. Place sesame seeds, almonds and pumpkin seeds in a large dry skillet. Over medium, heat, stir until contents are medium brown. Place contents of pan in blender. Blend until smooth. Leave almond mixture in blender. Add tortilla chips to blender with almond mixture. Blend until pulverized. Keep mixture in blender. In a saucepan saute onions and garlic. Add to blender. Add tomatoes, chicken broth, lime juice, cinnamon, chocolate and peppers. Blend until smooth. Pour over chicken. Preheat oven to 375 degrees. Cover and bake 1 hour. Place chicken on serving platter, pour sauce over chicken. Thin sauce with chicken broth if desired, before serving.

Serves 6-8

Spicy Shish-Kebabs

Alambres con Especias

3 pounds cubed beef (sirloin, chuck or round)
8 ounces red hot sauce (see recipe)
1 cup oil
1/3 cup red wine vinegar
3 garlic cloves
Optional:
2 teaspoons cumin
3 tablespoons soy sauce

Combine all ingredients and marinate meat 8-12 hours or overnight. String cubes of meat on skewer and charcoal broil about 15 minutes.

Serves 6-8

Chicken in Green Sauce

Pollo en Salsa Verde

1 whole chicken, sectioned
2 serrano peppers
10 small green or red tomatoes
1/2 banana
1 slice of bread
2 garlic cloves, crushed
Sprigs of coriander
Pinch of cumin, crushed
Salt and pepper to taste
3 tablespoons cooking oil
Optional:
1 teaspoon sugar

Boil chicken. In a separate pot, boil peppers and tomatoes. In a blender, add tomatoes, peppers, banana, bread, garlic and coriander. Blend on high until smooth.

In a skillet, add oil, and sauce out of the blender and then add the chicken. Salt and pepper to taste. Add the crushed cumin and stir. Simmer for 10 minutes. Add sugar if desired. Serve with long grain rice.

Serves 4-5

Chicken in Green Sauce

Pollo en Salsa Verde

1/3 cup all purpose flour
1 teaspoon paprika
1 1/4 teaspoon salt
1/4 teaspoon pepper
1 whole chicken, sectioned
3 tablespoons cooking oil
1 (2 ounce can) green tomatoes, drained and rinsed
1 (4 ounce can) green peppers, rinsed, seeded and sliced
1/4 cup chicken broth
1/4 cup onion, chopped
1/4 cup walnuts
1/4 cup almonds
Coriander, fresh sprigs, or 1/4 teaspoon dried
Dash pepper

Combine flour, paprika, teaspoon salt and pepper in plastic bag; add 2 or 3 pieces of chicken at a time and shake to coat. In a skillet heat oil until a drop of water sizzles. Brown chicken over medium heat for 15-20 minutes, turning pieces as necessary to brown evenly. Reduce heat and cover. Cook 30-40 minutes or until tender. Uncover during the last 10 minutes of cooking. Meanwhile, in blender combine remaining ingredients until pureed. Transfer sauce to 1 1/2 quart saucepan; heat thoroughly. To serve, arrange chicken pieces on platter and spoon sauce over.

Serves 3-4

Chicken and Squash

Calabaza con Pollo

1 small chicken fryer, sectioned
3-4 small, round squash, sliced
1/2 dozen fresh zucchini squash, sliced
2 ears fresh corn, cut or 1 medium can whole kernel corn,
*   drained*
3 tablespoons oil
1 large onion, minced
3 garlic cloves, minced
3 sprigs coriander, chopped
2 tomatoes, chopped
1/4 teaspoon cumin, crushed

Place chicken in large covered pot. Over high heat, bring to a boil, add a few peppers, reduce heat, cover and boil for 20 minutes. Remove pieces and drain. Reserve stock.

While chicken is cooking, trim off corn kernels.

In a Dutch oven heat 1 tablespoon oil, onions, garlic, corn and coriander. Saute until onion softens. Add chicken and saute until brown. Add tomato and continue cooking. If this starts to dry, do not add oil, add chicken stock liquid to moisten. When chicken is browned, add squash, salt, pepper and cumin and more stock just to cover. (Do not add too much liquid or you will have a soup instead of a stew.) Cook over low heat until chicken is tender. Serve immediately with hot tortillas.

Serves 5

Chicken and Zucchini

Calabaza con Pollo

1 chicken, sectioned
2 tablespoons oil
4 cups summer squash or zucchini, cubed
1/2 teaspoon cumin seed, crushed
3 garlic cloves, crushed
1/2 cup onion, diced
1 tomato, diced
1/4 cup bell pepper, diced
1/2 cup water
Salt and pepper to taste

Brown chicken in skillet with oil. Drain and add all other ingredients. Bring to boil; simmer for 20-30 minutes.

Serves 5

Chicken with Rice

Arroz con Pollo

6 green onions, sliced
1/2 cup olive oil (or other cooking oil)
2 (2 1/2 pound) chicken, fryers
1 teaspoon salt
1/2 teaspoon pepper
1/2 cup flour
6 fresh tomatoes, diced
2 cups chicken stock
2 cups long grain rice
Optional:
1/2 teaspoon saffron
2 green peppers
1/2 cup sherry

Saute onions in oil and remove from pan. Brown chicken pieces in sauce pan after dredging them in the flour, salt and pepper. When brown, add cooked onions, tomatoes, stock and saffron. Simmer covered until almost done. Add rice and cook 25 minutes longer. Just before serving, add sherry and green pepper.

Serves 6-8

Conchita's Spare Ribs

Costillas de Puerco

12 pounds pork spare ribs
1 tablespoon garlic powder
Seasoned salt and pepper to taste
1 quart applesauce
1 1/2 quarts mild barbecue sauce
1 tablespoon liquid smoke
Caraway seeds

Preheat oven to 325 degrees. Season the ribs with garlic powder, seasoned salt and pepper and place them in large shallow baking pans. Cover with foil and bake for 1 hour. Meanwhile, mix applesauce, barbecue sauce, liquid smoke and caraway seeds in a large sauce pan. Simmer 10-15 minutes. Brush ribs with sauce. Bake, uncovered for 30 minutes longer or preheat broiler, brush baked ribs with sauce. Serve with any remaining sauce.

Serves 6-8

Mexican Style Pork

Carne de Puerco a la Mexicana

1 pound deboned pork steaks*
1/2 yellow onion, peeled and sliced
1 green pepper, deveined and sliced
2 tablespoons peanut oil
2 garlic cloves, crushed
1/4 teaspoon ground cumin
1/4 teaspoon oregano
Salt to taste
2 tablespoons dry sherry

Cut the pork steaks into thin slices. Saute the pork quickly in oil and garlic. Add the onion and pepper and continue to fry. Add the cumin and oregano. Add salt. Add the sherry just before serving.

*1 pound meat can be substituted for pork.

Serves 3-4

Fried Pork

Asado de Puerco

1 pound pork meat, cubed
1-2 bay leaves
1 teaspoon thyme
4 ancho peppers
1 piece of toast
3 garlic cloves, crushed
1 teaspoon vinegar
Pinch of cloves
Salt and pepper to taste

Brown the meat with whole bay leaves and thyme. Drain excess oil and reserve.

In a separate pot bring water to a boil adding the peppers. After a few minutes remove peppers from pot. Skin and devein the peppers. Reserve water from peppers. In a blender add the peppers, toast, garlic, vinegar and a little water from the peppers together and puree.

Heat the drippings with the sauce. Add cumin, salt, pepper and cloves. Simmer for 10 minutes. Pour sauce over pork. Remove bay leaves and thyme.

Serves 4

Pork and Squash

Calabaza con Puerco

2 pounds pork steaks or roast, cubed
1 onion, diced
1 garlic clove, crushed
Pinch of cumin, crushed
1 can whole kernel corn
3 sprigs coriander
1 tomato, cubed
6 baby squash, sliced

Brown the pork until medium cooked. Add the onion, garlic, corn, coriander, and tomato and saute on lower heat. Next, add the squash and a little water and the spices and cook until squash is tender.

Serves 4-6

Pork Chops

Carne Adovada

3 pounds lean boneless center-cut chops, thinly sliced
1/3 cup chili powder
1-2 tablespoons red pepper flakes, crushed
2 garlic cloves, crushed
1 1/2 tablespoons ground cumin
1 1/2 tablespoons whole dried oregano
1 teaspoon salt
3 cups water
Lettuce, shredded
Sour cream or yogurt
Hot flour tortillas
Optional:
Orange juice
Onions

Trim and discard fat from chops. Place chops in a baking dish. Combine chili powder with red pepper flakes, garlic, cumin, oregano, salt and water; pour over chops, turning chops to coat. Cover and refrigerate at least 8 hours, turning the chops occasionally. Bake covered at 325 degrees for 1 hour; uncover and bake 1 to 1 1/2 hours, spooning marinade over chops occasionally. Cool to room temperature; shred meat with fingers and return to baking dish. Bake at 350 degrees for 30 minutes or until most of water is absorbed and meat is saucy. Serve with shredded lettuce, sour cream or yogurt and hot flour tortillas.

Serves: 6

Pork El Paso

Calabaza con Carne de Puerco

1 pound of pork meat, cubed
4 medium squash, cubed
1/2 onion, cubed
2 large tomatoes or 1/2 can tomato sauce
3 garlic cloves, crushed
Pinch of crushed cumin
Salt and pepper to taste
1 jalapeno pepper, sliced

Brown meat. Drain excess oil when browned. Saute onions, tomatoes, jalapenos, squash, garlic and cumin. Stir. Add meat and water to mixture and let simmer for 15 minutes. Add salt and pepper to taste.

Serves 2-4

Pork Stuffing for Burritos

Chilorio

2 pounds pork shoulder, cubed
Hot water
5 ancho peppers (see glossary)
4 garlic cloves
1/8 teaspoon cumin
1/4 teaspoon oregano
6 peppercorns
1/3 cup vinegar
Oil or lard

Cover the meat with water in a frying pan; add salt and bring to a boil, uncovered. Lower heat and allow the meat to cook until dry. Turn it frequently until brown. After cooking, at least 45 minutes, shred the meat .

Sauce: Seed and devein the peppers. Let them soak in water for 10-15 minutes. Place peppers, garlic, cumin, oregano, peppercorns and vinegar in a blender. Blend until smooth. The sauce will be a thick paste.

If there is no fat left from cooking the meat in the frying pan, add some oil or lard. Mix the meat and the chili sauce together in the frying pan. Cook on low heat for about 20 minutes, stirring frequently. The result will be a dry filling that is most often used in burritos. Will fill 10-12 tortillas.

Serves 6-8

Smothered Pork

Tapado de Cerdo

3 pounds boneless pork loin, cubed
6 dried pasilla peppers (see glossary)
3 garlic cloves
4 tablespoons lard
1 large onion, chopped
3 large tomatoes, peeled, seeded and chopped
1 (10 ounce can) green tomatoes
Salt and pepper to taste
3 Mexican sausage links (chorizo)
4 ounces boiled ham, chopped
1 ounce slivered almonds
2 ounces pimiento-stuffed green olives
1/2 cup dry sherry

Cook pork in salted water, barely covering the pork, until tender, or about 2 hours. Pour off stock and reserve. Seed and devein peppers and soak them in 1 cup of hot water for an hour. Add peppers and garlic in blender and enough of the water in which they soaked, to form a thick paste when blended. Heat 2 tablespoons lard in skillet and fry paste for 5 minutes, stirring constantly. Cool and mix with pork. Put into heavy sauce pan. Heat remaining lard in a skillet and saute onion; add all of the tomatoes, reserving liquid. Cook until sauce is smooth and thick, adding liquid from tomatoes as necessary. Season with salt and pepper and set aside. Remove sausage from casing, slice and saute. Drain and cover pork with a layer of sausage followed by a layer of ham, almonds and olives. Pour on sauce and then pour on sherry. Cook, covered over low heat stirring frequently to prevent burning; or bake in a 350 degree oven for 30 minutes.

Serves 6

Marinated Shish-Kebab

Alambres y Escabeche

1 cup escabeche*
1/2 cup chopped jalapenos
1/4 cup red wine vinegar
1 teaspoon garlic salt
1 tablespoon tomato paste
1 1/2 pounds cubed sirloin, chuck or round

Blend all ingredients and place meat in marinade and refrigerate overnight. Skewer meat and broil over charcoal fire about 15 minutes. Baste during cooking time with melted butter if meat is very lean.

*Escabeche can be jalapeno pickling brine.

Serves 4-6

Meatballs

Albondigas

1 pound ground beef*
1 egg
1 onion, chopped
1/4 cup coriander*
1/2 cup uncooked rice
1 cup tomato, chopped
1/2 teaspoon cumin powder or fresh ground
3-4 garlic cloves
1 1/2 cups water

Combine meat, egg, onion, coriander and rice and shape into meatballs. In skillet, pour tomato, spices and water and bring to boil. Place meatballs in boiling mixture and simmer for 15-20 minutes. Serve with rice and tortillas.

*Salmon or tuna could easily be substituted for the beef; and yerba buena and mint could be substituted for the coriander.

Serves 4

B-B-Q Beef Skirts

Fajitas

3 pounds fajitas
1 cup cooking wine
1/2 cup mesquite flavor barbecue sauce
Oil
Optional:
Bell peppers
Onions

Preheat oven to 400 degrees. Brush oil on both sides of fajitas. Mix wine and barbecue sauce together, and brush on fajitas as well. Bake for 30 minutes. Cut fajitas against the grain. Serve with tortillas.

May be garnished with bell peppers and onions while baking.

Serves 4-6

Beef Rolls

Rollitos de Carne

1 pound ground beef
1 pound stew beef, uncut, 1/2 inch thick
1 (12 ounce) can mixed vegetables
2 medium potatoes, cubed and boiled
1 (12 ounce) can tomato sauce
1 package seasoning mix for beef
Dash of meat tenderizer
Black pepper
Garlic, whole or powder
Salt
1 medium bell pepper
1 medium onion

Preheat oven to 250 degrees. In a skillet brown ground beef in a small amount of water; add salt and pepper to taste. Cover and simmer. Drain ground beef, stir in vegetables and add potatoes. On a cutting board, cut beef into strips 3-4 inches wide by 7 inches long. Add meat tenderizer, pepper, garlic and salt to all strips. Put ground beef mixture in the center of each strip and roll up, holding it together with a toothpick. Place all the beef rolls into a baking pan. Sprinkle with season mix and pour tomato sauce over the rolls. Garnish with bell pepper and sliced onion. Place in oven and cook for 20-30 minutes or until brown.

Serves 2-4

Mexican Beef Sandwich Rolls

1 can sliced olives, drained
1 (7 ounce can) green pepper sauce
1/4 teaspoon ground cumin
1/4 teaspoon salt
1/2 teaspoon chili powder
6 rectangular french rolls
1/2 pound lean ground beef
1 onion, chopped
1/4 pound sliced mushrooms
4 ounces cheddar cheese, sliced
4 ounces Monterrey Jack cheese, sliced
6 slices crisp bacon

Cut rolls in half lengthwise; scoop out most of the insides. Lightly toast cut sides; set aside. Crumble beef into frying pan over medium heat and brown; add onion and mushrooms and saute. Stir in olives, pepper sauce, cumin, salt and chili powder; simmer until liquid is absorbed. Arrange cheddar cheese on one half of each roll. Top each with 1 slice of bacon, 1/6 of meat mixture and the Monterrey Jack cheese. Add to other half of roll; wrap each sandwich in foil. Chill if making ahead. Heat in 375 degree oven for 12-15 minutes (30 minutes if chilled).

Serves 6

Spicy Beef

Picadillo

2 carrots, peeled and cubed
1 potato, peeled and cubed
1 1/2 pounds ground beef
Oil to fry
1/2 onion, cubed
2 tomatoes
1 garlic clove, crushed
Pinch of cumin, crushed
1 teaspoon vinegar
Salt
Pepper

Boil carrots and potatoes until tender. In a skillet add oil and saute onion with the beef. Brown the meat. In a blender add tomatoes, garlic, cumin and vinegar. Blend and pour this mixture over meat. Once the vegetables are cooked, drain the water and add vegetables to the meat. Stir and add salt and pepper to taste. Serve hot with tortillas and rice.

Serves 4

Meat and Gravy

Carne Guisada

1 cup canned tomatoes
1 garlic clove
1 teaspoon cumin
1 teaspoon peppercorn
1 thick round or T-bone steak, cubed
1/2 small onion, chopped
1 small bell pepper, chopped
1 cup water
Salt to taste
Bacon drippings
Optional:
Flour

Put tomatoes through blender; set aside. Grind spices in *molcajete* or in a blender. Brown meat in bacon drippings or small amount of shortening. Add onion and bell pepper, saute. Drain off grease. Stir in spices, tomatoes, water and salt. Partially cover skillet and simmer 30-40 minutes. More water may be needed if mixture becomes too dry.

Flour may be added for texture. Poorer cuts of meat can be used with this dish due to the longer cooking time. Two additional cloves of garlic and 1/2 teaspoon of cumin might be added.

Serves 4

Meat in Tomato Sauce

Carne en Salsa de Tomate

1 whole round steak
1 garlic clove or 1 tablespoon ground garlic
1/2 tablespoon cumin (whole or ground)
1/2 tablespoon peppercorns or 1/4 tablespoon ground
*   pepper*
1/4 small onion, chopped
Salt to taste
1 cup tomato sauce
1/4 cup water
Optional:
Fresh or canned picante sauce

Cut steak into portion sizes. Lightly fry. Add salt, onion, garlic, cumin and pepper. Add water, tomato sauce and picante sauce, if desired. Let meat simmer in tomato sauce mixture until water is cooked off to taste. Serve with corn or flour tortillas.

Serves 4-6

Shish-Kebabs

Alambres

2 pounds cubed meat (shoulder, butt or back strap)
1 part red wine vinegar
3 parts water
3 serrano peppers
Salt to taste
Whole black peppercorns
3 garlic cloves
Pinch of oregano
Pinch of cumin

Put all ingredients, except meat, in blender and blend well. Pour over meat and marinate 6-8 hours covered, or overnight.

Put meat on skewers. Add bacon grease to remaining marinade and use as baste while cooking, over hot charcoal fire. The bacon grease provides extra flavor and smokes the meat.

Serves 4-6

Bacon-Studded Roast

Carne Clavetada

3 pound brisket
5 slices bacon, cut in pieces
2 tablespoons slivered almonds
3/4 cup water
1 (4 ounce) can green peppers, rinsed, seeded and chopped
2 tablespoons vinegar
2 garlic cloves, minced
1 teaspoon salt
1/8 teaspoon pepper
1/4 teaspoon ground cinnamon
1/4 teaspoon dried thyme, crushed
1/4 teaspoon dried marjoram, crushed
1/4 teaspoon dried oregano, crushed
1/8 teaspoon ground cloves
2 tablespoons cooking oil
4 large potatoes, peeled and cubed

Trim fat from roast; cut small slits in the top surface of the brisket. Stud with bacon pieces and almonds. In bowl, combine water, peppers, vinegar, garlic, salt, pepper, cinnamon, thyme, marjoram, oregano and cloves. In large Dutch oven brown brisket on both sides in hot cooking oil. Pour chili mixture over meat. Bring to boil. Reduce heat and simmer, covered, for 1 3/4 hours. Add potatoes and additional water, if needed. Cover; simmer 45 minutes more or until potatoes are tender. Transfer meat and potatoes to serving platter; discard juices.

Serves 6

Fried Goat

Cabrito Guisado

Usually a whole *cabrito* is cut up with a cleaver or saw into medium sized pieces (including the bone) and then stewed in a large dutch oven or other heavy stew pot.

2 large yellow onions
1 head of garlic, crushed
1 tablespoon salt
2 teaspoons ground pepper
2-3 tablespoons ground cumin
2 medium green bell peppers, chopped
2-3 hot peppers, chopped or diced
3 diced tomatoes, fresh
Oil or shortening

Lightly saute onion, peppers and garlic to add taste to oil. Remove and set aside. Increase heat, add cut up cabrito and brown well. Drain off excess oil if any. Add sauteed vegetables and tomato and a little hot water to further saute. Add salt, pepper and cumin, mix in well. When thoroughly mixed, add enough hot water to barely cover meat and bring to boil. Stir and reduce heat to simmer; cover. Cook until tender. If it's too watery, thicken with flour or corn starch. Taste for seasoning. **Important Note:** All goat is strong tasting, even when young and tender. That is the reason a large amount of cumin is used. Long peppers can be used instead of hot peppers.

To make "*Cabrito Fritada*" use the goat's blood as an ingredient.

Serves 6-8

Baby Goat Broiled by Coals

Cabrito al Pastor

7-8 pound goat
1/8 teaspoon salt
Optional:
Corn or flour tortillas

Normally a whole *cabrito* is broiled at once on a double cross-shaped metal spit which holds all four legs open. The spit is inserted to the side of the coals so that any drippings do not fall into the fire and the heat is indirect rather than direct. Nothing more than salt is added. The meat is done when golden brown. Serve with corn or flour tortillas.

Serves 6-8

Roasted Goat

Cabrito

7-8 pound goat, sectioned
2 bell peppers, sliced
3 medium onions, sliced
3-4 carrots, sliced
3 sticks margarine
3 garlic cloves
Lime juice
5 tablespoons Worcestershire sauce
Salt and pepper to taste

Place the goat in the bottom of a large roasting pan. Add salt and pepper as desired. Place vegetables on top of meat. Make a sauce of the margarine, garlic, lime juice and Worcestershire sauce and put aside. During the last hour, baste the meat about every ten minutes with this sauce. Cooking time for the goat is 2-3 hours, or until tender. Cook with the roasting pan cover on during the first two hours.

Serves 6-8

Goat

Cabrito

7-8 pound cabrito
Garlic salt
Pepper
Oregano
Optional:
BBQ sauce
Onion slices

Rub with garlic salt, pepper and oregano. If barbecuing, baste every hour or so with barbecue sauce. If baking in oven, add onion slices to meat and serve with barbecue sauce.

Goat is very tender meat, sweet and succulent, but it can be overcooked so keep testing for doneness. *Cabrito* is the meat of a young milk-fed goat. It is generally cooked split in half and charcoal broiled. If oven baking, brown at 500 degrees, and then reduce heat to 350 degrees and cook 18 minutes to the pound.

Serves 6-8

Turkey

Pavo

4-5 pound turkey breast*
1 teaspoon salt
2 tablespoons lard or bacon drippings
2 medium tomatoes, peeled, seeded and chopped
1 medium onion, chopped
2 green peppers, rinsed, seeded and chopped
1/2 cup almonds
1/3 cup raisins
1 corn tortilla, sectioned
2 tablespoons sesame seeds
1 garlic clove
1/2 teaspoon crushed dried red pepper
1/4 teaspoon salt
Pepper to taste
1/4 teaspoon anise seed, crushed
1/4 teaspoon ground cloves
1/4 teaspoon ground cinnamon
1/4 teaspoon coriander
1/2 square unsweetened chocolate, melted

Simmered method: In large Dutch oven combine turkey breast, salt and enough water to cover. Bring to boil. Reduce heat and simmer 1 1/4 hours or until meat is tender. Drain, reserving 1 1/2 cups broth. Cool turkey slightly. Pat dry with paper towel. In same Dutch oven melt lard. Brown breast in lard. Drain off excess fat. In blender combine the reserved broth, tomatoes, onion, peppers, almonds, raisins, tortilla, sesame seeds, garlic, red pepper, salt, pepper, anise seed, cloves, cinnamon and coriander.

Blend until finely chopped. Stir in chocolate. Pour over turkey breast in Dutch oven. Cover and simmer for 20 minutes or until hot. To serve, slice turkey breast, arrange on platter, spooning sauce on top.

Roasting method: Place turkey breast on a rack in a shallow roasting pan. Omit salt and lard. Cover loosely with foil. Bake in a 325 degree oven for 3 hours. In blender container combine the reserved broth, tomatoes, onion, peppers, almonds, raisins, tortilla, sesame seed, garlic, red pepper, salt, pepper, anise seed, cloves, cinnamon and coriander. Blend until finely chopped. Stir in chocolate. Transfer to sauce pan. Bring to boil. Cover and simmer 10 minutes. Serve over slices of roasted turkey breast.

*Chicken could be substituted for turkey

Serves 8-10

Beef Intestines

Tripas

10 pounds beef intestines
Salt

Rinse well and cut into 4 inch pieces. Boil in Dutch oven until fat rises. Drain. Brown in skillet until dry and crispy. Sprinkle with salt. May also be baked in oven or barbecued on the grill.

Serves 6-8

Mexican Pheasant

2 pheasants
1 onion, chopped
Serrano peppers, chopped
2 large tomatoes, boiled and diced
1 (8 ounce) can tomato sauce
2 teaspoons chili powder
1 (16 ounce) can red kidney beans, drained
Corn tortilla chips

2 cups cheese of choice, shredded

Boil and debone pheasants. Chop or grind the pheasant meat. Add pheasant, onion and peppers together in iron skillet and saute. Add diced tomatoes, tomato sauce, chili powder and beans. Cover and cook for about one hour. Serve on top of chips, garnished with cheese.

Serves 2-4

Wild Duck in Red Wine

2 wild ducks
2 carrots
2 celery stalks
2 onions
4 tablespoons tomato paste
4 slices bacon
3/4 pound mushrooms
1 pint red wine
2 tablespoons flour
2 tablespoons butter (softened)
1/2 cup green olives
Salt
Pepper

Grate the carrots and chop the celery and onions; wipe the ducks, season with salt and pepper, fill center cavity with the vegetables and place bacon on the breast. Place on a roasting rack and bake in the oven preheated to 350 degrees for 35 minutes. Remove duck from pan and when it's cool enough to handle, cut into serving pieces. Cut the bacon into small pieces and place back in roasting pan with carrots, onions, celery and the drippings. Mix the flour with butter, stir it into the sauce, add olives, salt and pepper and bake for 30 minutes. Serve with rice.

*Contrary to popular belief, wild duck isn't hard to cook, it's just hard to get. This is one way to prepare it but you might prefer to just roast it with herbs or try your own sauce. Fruits are very complementary to the rich duck flavor. Glaze it with marmalade and garnish with hot orange slices. Do not let the ducks get too dry.

Serves 2-4

Grilled Venison Steaks

1 (12 to 14 pound) venison hindquarter
1 (16 ounce) bottle Italian dressing
1 (2.75 ounce) package dry onion mix
3/4 cup butter or margarine, melted
2 teaspoons pepper

Separate each muscle of the hindquarter, and cut away from bone. Slice each muscle across the grain into 1 inch thick slices (reserve remaining meat for use in another recipe). Remove and discard the white membrane surrounding each steak. Combine salad dressing and soup mix in a large shallow dish, stirring well; add steaks. Cover and marinate steaks in refrigerator for 1 hour, turning once. Combine butter and pepper, stirring well; set aside. Remove steaks from marinade. Grill about 5 inches from hot coals 8-10 minutes on each side or until done, basting occasionally with butter mixture.

Serves 10-12

Lamb Stew

1 1/2 pounds lamb
1 slice ham
1 garlic clove
2 tablespoons almonds
Cloves
4 tomatoes, skinned
1 cup sherry wine
Vinegar
3 peppers, of choice
2 tablespoons raisins
Pepper and salt to taste
Oil

Section lamb and cut ham into strips and lay on top of lamb. Add diced garlic, soaked almonds and cloves. Place in a pot or kettle. Add the tomatoes, wine, vinegar, peppers, raisins, oil and salt and pepper. Cook over medium heat until tender.

Serves 4

Cow's Tongue

Lengua

1 whole tongue
All season mix
1/2 onion, diced
1/2 bell pepper, diced
Salt and pepper
Corn tortillas
2 lemons
Salt and pepper to taste

Prepare tongue by smothering with seasoning. In a crockpot place tongue, onion, bell pepper and fill half way with water. Add salt, pepper and more seasoning to water. Cook overnight on low for about 6 hours. Once it is cooked, take the tongue out of the water. Peel the outer layer of the tongue and shred finely. Serve on corn tortillas with picante sauce. Also add a squeeze of lemon and a dash of salt to each taco.

Serves 8-10

Beef Brain Filling

Relleno de Sesos

1 onion
3 tablespoons butter
1 set of cooked beef brains, chopped
Sprig of nutmeg or goosefoot
Serrano or jalapeno pepper
Salt
Pepper
2 1/2 cups tortilla dough (see recipe)

Saute one finely chopped onion in butter until tender. Add the beef brains and cook until golden. Add a sprig of goosefoot or a pinch of nutmeg and a small chopped pepper. Cook 2-3 minutes. Mixture should be quite dry. Use to stuff tortillas. Fold over and seal the edges. Fry in oil. Drain on paper towels and serve hot.

These turnovers can be unbaked tortillas stuffed with a variety of fillings. Leftover *picadillo, mole*, beans, sardines or any other meat can be used. For a main course, use the small (4 inch) tortilla. For cocktails, use the half size one.

Serves 6

Mexican Sausage

Chorizo

1 pound coarse-ground lean pork
1 teaspoon salt
2 tablespoons chili powder
1/4 teaspoon cloves
1/2 teaspoon cinnamon
1 tablespoon paprika
1 garlic clove, crushed
1 teaspoon oregano
2 tablespoons cider vinegar
2 tablespoons water

Combine all ingredients. Stuff into casings or fry plain (best in casings). For breakfast it is great when mixed with eggs, refried beans or potatoes.

Yield: 1 pound

SEAFOOD

Shrimp with Tomato and Onion

Camarones Rancheros

3 tablespoons butter
15 medium shrimp, chopped
1 tomato, chopped
1/2 medium onion, chopped
1 tablespoon coriander
Salt and pepper to taste
1 cup water
Optional:
2-3 jalapeno or serrano peppers, chopped

Saute shrimp with butter for about 3 minutes until almost cooked. Add remaining ingredients. Add water and simmer for 5 minutes.

Serves 2-3

Shrimp Fajitas

Fajitas de Camarones

1 pound shrimp, peeled and butterflied
1 onion, sliced
1 bell pepper, sliced
1 tomato, sliced
1 teaspoon black pepper
1 teaspoon garlic salt
1 cup soy sauce
1 cup water
3 tablespoons butter

Mix first eight ingredients, and marinate for 2 hours. Drain. Saute onions, bell pepper and tomato in butter until tender. Remove from pan. Cook shrimp in same pan for 3-5 minutes, just until done, without adding any more butter. Serve onions, bell pepper and tomato, then place shrimp on top.

Serves 4-5

Fried Shrimp

Camarones Fritos

1 pound raw shrimp, shelled and deveined
Oil for frying
3/4 cup flour
1 egg, well beaten
1/2 cup water
1/2 teaspoon salt
1/4 teaspoon baking powder
1 teaspoon grated onion

Cold Sauce:
1/4 cup mayonnaise
2 tablespoons sour cream
2 teaspoons horseradish

Mix sauce ingredients and chill. Butterfly shrimp, leaving tails intact. Wash well. Dry on paper towel. In a deep mixing bowl, combine the egg and water. Sift the flour, salt and baking powder into the bowl. Add the grated onion. Beat with a wire whisk or rotary eggbeater until the batter is smooth, or 2-3 minutes. Heat the oil to 370 degrees. Dip the shrimp in the batter. Place them one by one gently into the fat. Fry until light brown, turning once during frying. Drain fried shrimp on paper towel. Sprinkle with salt. Serve with cold sauce, tartar sauce, or picante sauce.

Serves 2

Shrimp Fricassee

Pipian de Camarones

2 pounds large shrimp
1/2 cup shelled pumpkin seeds
1 small onion
2 garlic cloves
6 sprigs fresh coriander
1/2 pound tomatoes, peeled and seeded
6 pequin peppers or to taste
1/2 tablespoon ground coriander seeds
3 whole canned pimientos, chopped
Salt and pepper to taste
1/2 teaspoon sugar
3 tablespoons salad oil
1 tablespoon lemon juice

Cook shrimp for 5 minutes in boiling water; cool and peel; reserve water. Pour pumpkin seeds in a blender and blend as finely as possible. Reserve. Put onion, garlic, coriander, tomatoes, peppers and coriander seeds in blender. Blend to a smooth sauce. Add ground pimiento, salt, pepper, sugar and pumpkin seeds. Heat oil in skillet and cook mixture for 5 minutes, stirring constantly. Thin with about 1 cup of the reserved shrimp water to make a thick sauce. Add shrimp and heat briefly, stirring without letting sauce come to a boil. Add lemon juice.

Serves 6

Shrimp Croquettes

Torta de Camaron

4 eggs, separated
2 ounces dried powdered shrimp
1/2 cup pinto beans, cooked and mashed
Oil for frying
Salt and pepper to taste

Beat egg whites until fluffy. Lightly beat yolks in a separate bowl. Add beans to yolks; season to taste. Fold into egg whites. Spoon mixture into hot oil (to make patties about 3 inches in diameter). Fry until brown. Drain and serve with *ensalada de nopalitos* (Cactus Salad).

Serves 4

Mexican Clams

Almejas

5 pounds raw clams, in shells
2 tomatoes, peeled and chopped
2 serrano peppers
1 onion, chopped
1 tablespoon coriander, chopped
3 tablespoons olive oil
Salt and pepper to taste
3 cups water

After washing the clams, place them in a large iron skillet. Add the remaining ingredients to the clams with the olive oil and three cups of water. Salt and pepper to taste. Cook over low heat until clams open. Discard any unopened clams. Drain and serve warm with melted butter.

Serves 6-8

Fish in Hazelnut Sauce

Pescado en Salsa de Avellanas

3 pounds fillets of any non-oily white fish
2 cups white wine court bouillon
3 ounces hazelnuts
3 tablespoons olive oil
1 slice thin white bread
1 garlic clove
1 bunch parsley
1 teaspoon saffron

Parboil fish in the court bouillon. Soak hazelnuts in hot water for a few minutes and remove skins. Heat olive oil in a skillet and fry the bread with the garlic. Put the bread, garlic, hazelnuts, parsley and liquid from poached fish in a blender. Blend to a smooth, medium-thick sauce. Add saffron and adjust seasoning. Put fish in a shallow casserole and cover with the sauce. Cover casserole and bake at 350 degrees for 20-30 minutes until fish is fully cooked.

Serves 6

Cod with Rice

Bacalao con Arroz

2 garlic cloves, crushed
1 onion, chopped
1 poblano pepper, roasted, deveined and chopped
1 bay leaf
1/2 teaspoon thyme
1 pound cod
2 tomatoes, peeled
Salt to taste
Pepper to taste
1 cup rice
2 cups broth
Saffron

Saute one garlic clove. Add onion and poblano pepper. Add bayleaf and thyme and stir in diced cod. Add peeled tomatoes. Salt and pepper to taste. Add rice and fry while stirring. Add broth and bring to boil. Add saffron with remaining crushed garlic. Cover, lower heat and cook until all liquid is absorbed. Remove bay leaf before serving.

Serves 4

Catfish with White Cheese

Barbo con Queso Blanco

2 onions, chopped
4 tablespoons butter or margarine
2 pounds catfish fillets
3/4 cup wine
3/4 cup water
Juice from 2 limes
2 tablespoons flour
2 cups whipping cream
1 garlic clove, crushed
Pinch of cumin, crushed
Salt to taste
Pepper
1 cup white cheese of choice

Saute the onions in 2 tablespoons butter. Remove from skillet and put aside. Place fish fillets in skillet and add wine, lime juice and water. Cover and cook on low for 5-7 minutes. Remove fish and place in oven broiler. Bring broth to boil and allow it to cook down to about 1 cup of liquid, which should take less than 10 minutes. Put the liquid aside. Melt 2 tablespoons butter in skillet. Stir in the flour, crushed garlic and pinch of cumin. Cook for 1 minute. Add the broth and stir in with cream. Stir in onions. Salt and pepper to taste. Spoon the sauce over the fish in the broiler and sprinkle freely with white cheese. Broil 2-3 minutes and serve.

Serves 4

Red Snapper in Dried Chili

Guachinango en Chile

2 red snappers
3 garlic pods
3 peppercorns
1 tablespoon achiote pepper seeds
Pinch of cumin
1/4 teaspoon oregano
1/4 teaspoon hot paprika
Salt to taste
1/4 cup orange juice or white vinegar
Olive oil for cooking

Remove head, tail and backbone of fish. Do not remove scales. Open and lay flat. Crush garlic, peppercorns, pepper seeds and cumin. Make a paste with this and the remaining ingredients; mix well. Spread paste all over fish and set aside for several hours. Brush seasoned side of the fish with olive oil and cook it seasoned side down over the charcoal or broiler for about 10 minutes. Turn over and cook on the skin side until fish is just cooked through.

Serves 2-4

Yucatan Fish

Pescado Yucateco

1 whole fish (pompano or snapper)
1 lemon
Salt and pepper to taste
4 tablespoons olive oil
1 onion, finely chopped
3 ounces green olives, chopped
1 ounce can pimientos, chopped with juice
1 teaspoon annatto
2 tablespoons fresh coriander or parsley
1 orange
2 hard-boiled eggs, chopped

Marinate fish for 15 minutes in lemon juice, salt and pepper.
Heat olive oil in a skillet and saute onion. Add olives,
pimiento with juice, annatto, coriander, salt and pepper.
Cook for a few minutes and add orange juice. Put fish in
buttered casserole, cover with sauce and cook in a 400
degree oven for 1/2 hour or until tender.

Serves 6

Red Snapper Veracruz

Guachinango a la Veracruzana

3 limes
6 ounces water
4 (8 ounce) red snapper fillets
Optional:
Trout, redfish or drum

Sauce:
3 ounces olive oil
2 garlic cloves, crushed
1 onion, finely chopped
1/3 cup green olives, pitted and sliced
3 tablespoons Spanish capers (plus a splash of vinegar from jar)
3 medium tomatoes, chopped
1 bay leaf
1 cup semi-dry white wine
1/2 long yellow pepper for decoration
Optional:
Chopped jalapenos

Squeeze lime juice into small bowl, mix with 6 ounces of water. Rub lime water over 4 fillets and leave marinating in refrigerator for 4 hours before cooking.

Sauce: Saute garlic, onion, olives, capers, tomatoes and bay leaf in oil. Add wine and let simmer on medium heat for 5 minutes or until sauce is slightly thick. For a hot and spicy flavor, add jalapenos and pickling brine to sauce and simmer.

Baking: Preheat oven to 350 degrees and place marinated fish side by side in large baking dish. Cover with sauce and bake for 15 minutes or until flaky.

This cholesterol-free dish goes great with white rice, broccoli or a vegetable of choice.

Serves 3-4

Shrimp and Bell Peppers

Camarones con Rajas

1 onion, finely chopped
2 garlic cloves, finely chopped
3 tablespoons oil
2 tomatoes, skinned, seeded and finely chopped
1 bell pepper , sliced in julienne strips
Salt and pepper to taste
1 pound shrimp, boiled and shelled

Saute onion and garlic. Add tomatoes, bell pepper, salt and pepper. Add shrimp and cook for 10 minutes.

Serves 2-4

Stuffed Red Snapper

Guachinango Relleno

4 small red snapper fish
4 limes
4 garlic cloves, crushed
Salt and pepper to taste
7 tablespoons butter
1 onion, chopped
3/4 pound tomatoes, diced
3/4 cup raw shrimp, peeled and deveined
3/4 cup raw scallops
1 tablespoon parsley
3/4 cup cooked crabmeat
1 1/2 tablespoons olive oil

The fish is normally cleaned and cooked with the head intact, but the head can be removed. Mix lime juice, garlic, salt and pepper into a paste. Rub each fish inside and out with this paste and marinate four to five hours.

Melt two tablespoons of butter and saute the onion until soft. Add the diced tomatoes and cook until thickened. Add chopped shrimp and scallops. Stir the parsley into the sauce and cook until tender. Add crabmeat and stir. Stuff each fish and close the pouch with toothpicks. Grease a baking dish with remaining butter; place fish in dish and cook under vented aluminum foil in a preheated oven at 350 degrees for 25-30 minutes or until fish is done.

Serves 4

Red Snapper

Guachinango

5-6 red snapper fillets
4 limes
1 teaspoon salt
1/2 teaspoon pepper
2 tablespoons vegetable oil
2 cups cream
1 cup slivered almonds
2/3 cup Monterrey Jack cheese, grated

Marinate fish with lime juice, pepper and salt for 1 hour. Saute fish in small amount of oil for 2-3 minutes. Place fish in baking dish. Pour cream over fish and sprinkle cheese and almonds over fish; bake in a 350 degree oven for 15 minutes.

Serves 4-5

DESSERTS

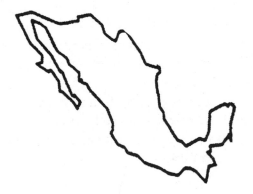

Sweet Tortilla Fritters

Bunuelos

2 eggs
1 cup milk
1 teaspoon salt
1 teaspoon baking powder
2 tablespoons sugar
4 cups flour
1/4 cup melted butter
Sugar and cinnamon

Beat eggs thoroughly. Whisk milk into eggs. Sift dry ingredients and add gradually to the egg-milk mixture; then add melted butter. Turn onto a lightly floured board and knead very gently until the dough is smooth. Roll out as thin as possible and cut into 2-3 inch squares or circles the size of a tortilla. Fry in very hot deep fat or oil (370 degrees) until delicately browned, turning as the first side puffs up. Roll in sugar and cinnamon. Store in an airtight container to keep fresh.

Yield: 3 dozen

Tortilla Fritters

Bunuelos

1 pound flour
1 tablespoon shortening
1/2 cup sugar
2 teaspoons cinnamon
1 cup milk
1/2 teaspoon salt
Oil to fry
1/2 cup brown sugar
Optional:
Honey

Mix flour, salt and shortening well. Add milk little by little and knead to desired consistency. Make small balls and roll out to a thin layer. Heat 1/4 inch of oil in a saucepan. Place each tortilla into pan and fry until golden brown on both sides. Set aside on paper towels to soak up excess oil.

In a plate mix sugar, cinnamon and brown sugar. Pass each *bunuelo* through this mixture. Dipping the tortilla fritters in honey can also be an option. When rolling out dough you can cut out different shapes for creativeness.

Yield: 3 dozen

Mexican Torte

2 large packages chocolate chips
3 pints sour cream
1/4 cup powdered sugar
10 large flour tortillas

Melt chocolate chips in double broiler, then mix with 4 cups of sour cream. In bowl, mix sugar with remaining 2 cups sour cream and set aside. On large platter, lay one tortilla flat, and evenly spread 1/8 of chocolate mixture. Repeat process for each of 8 tortillas. Add 9th tortilla and spread with 1/2 of sugar and sour cream. Add 10th tortilla and spread with remaining sugar and sour cream. Trim the uneven edges with knife and cover cake with large bowl inverted over it so that bowl does not touch cake. Refrigerate for at least 12 hours or overnight. Can be decorated with chocolate curls if desired. Cut in small wedges.

Serves 12

Sugar Tortillas

Gorditas de Harina de Azucar

1 pound flour
1/2 pound sugar
3/4 pound shortening
2 eggs
2 teaspoons vanilla
4 teaspoons baking powder
2 cups warm milk

In a large bowl sift the flour. In a separate bowl beat eggs. In the bowl with the sifted flour add eggs, shortening, vanilla and baking powder. Mix well. Add warm milk and knead into a ball until smooth. Make balls and roll out, these are supposed to be thick not thin. Heat a griddle until hot. Place a *gordita* on the griddle. Brown on each side. Serve warm with butter.

Yield: 2 dozen

Thelma's Sopapillas

4 cups flour
1 teaspoon baking powder
1/2 teaspoon salt
2 eggs
1 cup milk
2 tablespoons melted shortening, cooled slightly
Oil for deep-frying

Sift flour, baking powder and salt together. Beat eggs until light and add milk and shortening. Combine the 2 mixtures, using only as much of the flour as the liquid will absorb. Roll the dough out as thin as possible. Cut into 3x4 inch rectangles. Deep-fry in hot fat or oil until light brown. May be used as a bread or as a dessert served with honey.

Yield: 20-30 puffs

Fried Bread

Sopapillas

4 cups flour
1 1/2 teaspoons salt
1 teaspoon baking powder
1 tablespoon sugar
1 tablespoon shortening
1 cake yeast or 1 package dry yeast
1/4 cup warm water
1/4 cup scalded milk
Optional:
Honey
Powdered sugar

Combine the dry ingredients and fold in shortening. Dissolve yeast in warm water. Add to scalded milk that has cooled to room temperature. Make a well in center of dry ingredients. Pour liquid into well and work into dry ingredients to make dough. Knead dough 15-20 times and set aside for approximately 10 minutes.

Roll dough to 1/4 inch thickness or slightly thinner, then cut into squares or triangles and fry in melted shortening at 420 degrees. Fry only a few at a time so fat stays hot. Drain *sopapillas* on absorbent towels and serve as bread.

Top with honey and/or powdered sugar.

Yield: 20-30 *sopapillas*

Mexican Pastry

Molletes

Dough recipe:
1 packet yeast
1 cup warm water
1 tablespoon sugar
5-6 cups flour
1 cup milk, scalding
1 1/2 sticks butter, melted
3/4 cup sugar
3 eggs
2 teaspoons vanilla
2 teaspoons anise

Topping Recipe:
1 cup sugar
3/4 cup shortening
2 egg yolks
1/2 teaspoon baking powder
Pinch of salt
1 teaspoon vanilla
1 cup flour
2 egg whites

Dough: Mix yeast, sugar and water. Let stand for 10 minutes. In food processor, add 3 cups flour. Heat milk, add butter and sugar. Add yeast mixture to flour and process. Add milk mixture, eggs, anise and vanilla. Keep adding as much of the remaining flour as the processor can hold. Take out of processor and put into a large bowl. Keep adding flour until dough is smooth and holds shape. Knead for 3-5 minutes. Put into a buttered bowl and let rise for 1 hour. Punch down and shape into 3 inch diameter balls by 1 inch thick. Place 2 inches apart on greased cookie sheet. Put topping on each round, cover and let rise 1 hour or until doubled. Bake at 350 degrees for 15 minutes.

Topping: Mix shortening with sugar. Add the remaining ingredients, except egg whites. Divide mixture into 18 smooth balls and flatten. Brush egg whites on top of each *mollete* and place topping rounds over them.

Yield: 18 *molletes*

Sugar Cookies

Pan de Polvo

2 cups sugar
3 pounds shortening
5 pounds flour
Dash of salt
1 1/2 teaspoons cinnamon
3/4 cup anise tea

Boil anise tea and cool.

Mix shortening until fluffy, adding the sugar and tea slowly. Add salt and cinnamon. Put mixture in large mixing bowl. Add flour and form into 4 balls. Roll out 1/4 inch thickness and cut with small cookie cutter. Bake at 350 for about 15 minutes. Roll hot in sugar-cinnamon mixture and let cool.

Yield: 20 dozen

Mexican Sugar Cookies

Pan de Polvo

5 cups flour (sifted 5 times)
1 pound margarine
1 cup sugar
Cinnamon sugar for rolling

Before adding the flour, cream together margarine and sugar. Add flour and mix well. Make small balls and place on cookie sheet. Flatten with small glass, make round cookie and press criss-cross with fork. Bake at 350 degrees until light brown. Roll in cinnamon sugar.

Yield: 2 dozen

Mexican Sweets

Soletas

3 1/2 cups flour
3 1/2 cups sugar
4 egg yolks
4 egg whites
1 whole egg
1 cup butter

Beat the egg yolks, whole egg and sugar in dish until thick and soft peaks can be formed. In another dish, beat the egg whites until smooth. Combine the egg blends and sifted flour. Mix with folding motion. Butter baking tray and sprinkle with flour. Form in shape of pastries or use mold. Sprinkle sugar on top and bake for about 15 minutes.

Yield: 5 Dozen

Nut and Sugar Cookies

Galletas de Nues y Azucar

5 cups flour
2 cups lard
2 tablespoons baking powder
1 cup finely chopped nuts
1 cup brown sugar
1 teaspoon vanilla

Preheat oven to 350 degrees. Mix flour, baking powder, brown sugar, lard, vanilla and chopped nuts. Mix well and knead. Make little balls and set on greased cookie sheet. Bake for 20 minutes.

Yield: 3 dozen

Lenten Bread Pudding

Capirotada

1 teaspoon ground cinnamon or 3 sticks
2 1/2 cups raisins, diced apples and/or bananas
2 loaves white bread
3 cups shredded cheese
1 cup brown sugar
Optional:
1/2 cup pecan pieces

Boil raisins, sugar and cinnamon in water. In 4 quart size bowl place a layer of bread slices, cover with shredded cheese. Pour a ladle of hot boiled raisin mixture over bread and cheese. Continue layering in the same order. Cover with foil, allow to sit for 30 minutes. Serve warm. Add optional ingredients when serving.

Serves 10-12

Coffee Custard

Flan de Cafe

1 quart milk
10 level tablespoons ground coffee
4 whole eggs
1 egg, separated
1/2 cup sugar
1/2 teaspoon salt
1 teaspoon vanilla
Nutmeg
1 cup chopped walnuts
3 tablespoons guava jelly

Combine milk and coffee in saucepan. Bring to scalding point; remove from heat. Let stand 10 minutes, stirring occasionally. Strain through double layer of cheesecloth. Meanwhile beat 4 whole eggs and 1 egg yolk slightly; add sugar and salt. Add strained coffee mixture slowly, stirring constantly. Add vanilla. Pour into custard cups; sprinkle with nutmeg. Set cups in pan of cold water. Bake at 325 degrees for 50-60 minutes or until knife inserted near cup rim comes out clean. Remove from water. Chill. Top with chopped nuts. Beat egg white stiff; beat in guava jelly. Swirl over nuts.

Serves 6-8

Almond Custard

Flan Almendra

1/2 cup sugar
1 2/3 cup sweetened condensed milk
1 cup milk
3 eggs
3 egg yolks
1 teaspoon vanilla extract
1 cup slivered almonds, coarsely ground

Sprinkle sugar evenly in a 9 inch cakepan; place over medium heat. Using oven mitts, carmelize sugar by shaking pan occasionally until sugar is melted and a light golden brown; cool. (Mixture may crack slightly as it cools.) Combine remaining ingredients in container of electric blender; blend at high speed 15 seconds. Pour over caramelized sugar; cover pan with aluminum foil and place in a larger shallow pan. Pour about 1 inch of hot water into larger pan. Bake at 350 degrees for 55 minutes or until knife inserted near center comes out clean. Remove pan from water and uncover; let cool on wire rack at least 30 minutes. Loosen edges with a spatula. Place serving plate upside down on top of cake pan, quickly invert flan onto serving plate. Note: A little stirring may be necessary when caramelizing the sugar if a gas burner is used.

Serves 6-8

Caramel Custard

Leche Flan

Custard:
3 large eggs
2 large egg yolks
1/2 cup sugar
Pinch of salt
3 cups canned evaporated milk
1 1/2 teaspoons vanilla extract
Optional:
Butter for greasing
Caramel
1/2 cup sugar

Heat oven to 325 degrees. Pour about 1 inch hot water into a roasting pan large enough to hold a custard mold of about 5 cups capacity or 4 individual molds. Place pan in the oven.

Place the eggs and egg yolks into a bowl. Beat them lightly, but not to a froth. Mix in sugar and salt. Heat evaporated milk until hot. Slowly pour the hot milk into the bowl with the eggs, whisking vigorously. Mix in vanilla. If you are inverting the custard when serving, grease the custard mold or 4 individual molds with butter. Put sugar or caramel into a heavy frying pan, spreading it over the bottom. Heat over a medium heat. Do not stir. As the sugar melts and turns brown, tilt the pan around so that the sugar moves a little.

When all the sugar has caramelized, pour it into the custard mold (or divide it among the 4 individual molds). Tilt the mold(s) around so that the sides are coated as well as the bottom. The sugar will and should harden. Strain in the hot liquid custard and place the mold(s) in the roasting pan with water. Cook in the oven for 1 hour or until a knife inserted in the center of the custard comes out clean and the custard is set. If inverting, let it cool first. Serve warm or cold.

Serves 4

Baked Papaya

Papaya al Horno

4 cups ripened papaya pulp
1 cup shredded coconut
1 orange pulp, juice and grated rind
1 cup sugar
4 cups milk
4 eggs

Make a custard of the eggs, sugar, milk and orange. Place the papaya and coconut in a baking dish, cover with custard and bake at 350 degrees until firm and lightly browned.

Serves 4-6

Cinnamon Torte

Tortas de Canela

3/4 cup sugar
3/4 cup shortening
1/4 cup milk
1 1/2 cups flour
1 1/2 teaspoons baking powder
6 egg yolks
Filling:
1 cup sugar
1 cup water
1 teaspoon butter
1 heaping tablespoons cornstarch
Grated rind and juice of 1 lemon
1 egg
Topping:
6 egg whites, beaten stiff
1 cup sugar
1 tablespoon cinnamon
1/2 cup nuts

Cook filling ingredients and cool while baking torte. Mix sugar and shortening well. Add milk, flour, baking powder and egg yolks. Bake the torte. Spread lemon filling over the torte; then add topping and brown in oven.

Serves 10

Pumpkin Candy

Dulce de Calabaza

10 pounds mixed pumpkin
2 tablespoons lime
10 pounds sugar

Peel and cut pumpkin into pieces. Dip in lime for 2 hours. Take slices out and wash them with clear water. Cook in large pot with water. Take out and punch holes through them. Place back. Add 2 quarts water and 5 pounds of sugar. Keep temperature at boiling point. Cool for 15 minutes. Add remaining 5 pounds of sugar. Allow to sit overnight.

Put back to boil until all the water evaporates, about 2 hours (stringy stage). When sugar sticks to your finger it is ready. Tip pot and spoon syrup mixture over candy. Take out one by one and set on a large tray.

Yield: 8 dozen

Mexican Pecan Candy

Dulce de Nuez

2 cups sugar
3/4 cup milk
1/2 teaspoon baking soda
1 tablespoon margarine
1 1/2 teaspoons vanilla extract
1 1/2 cups pecan halves

Combine sugar, milk and soda in a large heavy saucepan; cook until a few drops form a soft ball when dropped in a saucer filled with cold water. Stir as little as possible. Remove from the heat; add margarine and vanilla. Beat until creamy. Stir in pecan halves. Sprinkle the baking soda onto the waxed paper and quickly drop the pecan mixture by spoonfuls onto paper to form patties. After candy has cooled, store in a covered dish.

Yield: 4 dozen

Burnt Milk Candy

Leche Quemada

2 quarts milk
1 pound sugar

Combine the milk and sugar in your heaviest saucepan and cook over moderate heat until the syrup shows signs of boiling. Reduce heat then to a slow-bubbling simmer and cook for about 2 hours or until the mixture leaves the sides of the pan. It should be a golden brown color and very smooth. Stir at constant, frequent intervals. When done, pour into a greased pan. Cool and cut into squares. A pecan half may be placed on each square.

Yield: 3 dozen

Candy Clusters

Penoche

2 cups sugar
2 cups milk
1 (7 ounce) jar marshmallow cream
1 (12 ounce) jar chunky style peanut butter
1 teaspoon vanilla

Combine sugar and milk, bring to a boil and cook for five minutes over medium heat to soft boil. Remove from heat. Add marshmallow cream, peanut butter and vanilla. Beat until well blended. Pour into 9 inch square greased pan. Cool and cut into squares.

Yield: 2 pounds

Papaya Fritters

Papayas Fritas

1 1/2 cups all purpose flour
2 1/2 teaspoons baking powder
3/4 teaspoon salt
1/2 teaspoon ground coriander
2/3 cup water
2 eggs
2 tablespoons oil
1 cup papaya cooked, drained and diced
Confectioners sugar
Oil for frying

Sift together flour, baking powder, salt and coriander. Pour water, eggs and oil into blender. Blend at high speed for 1 minute. Add papaya and egg mixture to flour. Stir until liquid and dry ingredients are blended. Heat 1/2 inch of oil in electric skillet, heated to 370 degrees. Drop in batter, a level tablespoon at a time, into oil. Brown on both sides. Drain fritters on absorbent paper. Just before serving, sift confectioners sugar on top of fritters. Serve with rum sauce.

Yield: 1 1/2 dozen

Rice Pudding

Atole de Arroz

1/2 cup white rice
1/2 cup evaporated milk
1/4 tablespoon salt
1/4 teaspoon cinnamon or 1 cinnamon stick*
1/2 cup sugar
Optional:
Raisins

Boil rice for about 30 minutes; if you are using the cinnamon stick, boil it with the rice. Do not drain. Add all other ingredients and simmer another 10 minutes. Stir gently. Sprinkle with raisins or cinnamon if desired.

*1/4 teaspoon of vanilla may be used instead of cinnamon.

Serves 4-6

Pineapple Pudding

Budin de Pina

1 pound finely chopped fresh pineapple*
4 ounces ground almonds
4 egg yolks, lightly beaten
1/2 to 1 cup sugar, depending on sweetness of pineapple
1/2 dry sherry
1/4 teaspoon ground cinnamon
12 lady fingers
Apricot jam
Sour cream
1 ounce slivered almonds

Mix pineapple, ground almonds, egg yolks, sugar, half the sherry and cinnamon. Cook over low heat, stirring constantly until thickened. Cool. Split the lady fingers and spread with a thin layer of apricot jam. Place half the lady fingers in the bottom of a serving dish. Sprinkle with half remaining sherry. Spread with half the pineapple mixture. Add second layer of ladyfingers, the rest of the sherry and the remaining pineapple mixture. Chill, spread with a layer of sour cream and stick with slivered almonds.

*Any canned or fresh fruit can be substituted for the pineapple.

Serves 8-10

Grandma's Pistachio Pie

Pie Shell:
2 cups flour
1 cup shortening
1/2 cup or more pecans
2 tablespoons water

Mix all ingredients together and spread in a pan. Cook at
450 degrees until shell is brown. Let it cool in refrigerator.

Pie Filling:
First layer:
1 cup cool whip
2 tablespoons cream cheese
Coconut
Second layer:
4 boxes pistachio pudding
6 1/2 cups milk, chilled

Mix cool whip and cream cheese and spread. Sprinkle
coconut. Make second layer by mixing pudding and milk.
Spread. Keep adding layers, sprinkle more coconut and top
with pecans.

Serves 4

Mango Sour Cream Pie

Pie Filling:
2 cups mangos, finely chopped
1/2 cup sugar
1/3 teaspoon salt
2 tablespoons flour
1 egg, beaten
1/2 teaspoon almond extract
1 cup sour cream
Prepared unbaked pastry shell
Topping:
1/2 cup white sugar
3/4 cup sifted flour
1/8 teaspoon salt
6 tablespoons butter

Chop mangos and set aside. Combine sugar, flour and salt. Add eggs, almond extract and sour cream. Beat until smooth. Add mangos, mix well and pour into pie shell. Bake at 375 degrees for 15 minutes. Remove pie from oven and reduce oven to 325 degrees. Meanwhile, mix all ingredients of topping together until crumbly. Sprinkle pie with topping and bake 40 minutes or until topping is slightly brown.

Serves 6

Mexican Chocolate Ice Cream

Nieve de Chocolate

3 eggs
1 cup sugar
2 quarts half-and-half
1 (16 ounce) can chocolate syrup
1/2 teaspoon ground cinnamon
1 tablespoon vanilla extract
1/4 tablespoon almond extract

Beat eggs at medium speed of until frothy. Gradually add sugar, beating until thick. Heat half-and-half in a 3 quart saucepan over low heat. Gradually stir about 1/4 of hot mixture into eggs; add to remaining hot mixture, stirring constantly. Cook over low heat until mixture is slightly thickened and reaches 165 degrees, stirring constantly. Remove from heat and stir in chocolate syrup and remaining ingredients. Cool in refrigerator. Pour into 1 gallon freezer can. Freeze according to manufacturer's instructions. Let ripen at least 1 hour.

Yield: 1 gallon

Pina Colada Cake

Pastel Pina Colada

1 box white cake mix
1/3 cup light rum or 1/3 cup pineapple juice
1/2 cup water
1/4 cup vegetable oil
4 eggs
1 package instant coconut cream pudding
1 cup flaked coconut
Icing:
1 package instant coconut cream pudding
1/3 cup light rum or 1/3 cup pineapple juice
8 ounces crushed pineapple with juice
8 ounces cool whip, thawed

Mix all ingredients together, adding coconut last. Beat 4 minutes. Pour into greased and floured 9x13 inch pan. Bake 30 minutes at 350 degrees.

Icing: Mix together first 3 ingredients. Fold in container of cool whip. Spread on cooled cake. Tastes best when prepared several hours before serving.

Serves 6-8

Mexican Wedding Cake

Pastel de Boda

Cake:
2 cups flour
2 teaspoons baking soda
2 eggs
1 large can pineapples with juice
1/4 teaspoon salt
2 cups sugar
2 teaspoons vanilla
1 cup chopped nuts
Frosting:
1/2 cup soft margarine (1 stick)
8 ounces cream cheese
1 cup powdered sugar, sifted
1 teaspoon vanilla

Cake: Beat all ingredients well and stir in nuts. Bake in 9x13 inch greased pan at 350 degrees for approximately 40 minutes. Let cool.
Frosting: Beat all ingredients until light and fluffy. Spread on evenly cake.

Serves: 8

Mexican Chocolate Cake

Torta de Chocolate

1/2 cup margarine
1/2 cup oil
2 squares unsweetened chocolate
1 cup water
2 cups unsifted all purpose flour
1 teaspoon baking soda
2 cups granulated sugar
1/2 cup sour milk*
2 eggs, beaten
1 teaspoon cinnamon
1 teaspoon vanilla extract

*Sour milk: Add 1 1/2 teaspoons vinegar in a 1 cup measure and fill with milk to measure 1/2 cup.

Heat oven to 350 degrees. Lightly grease a 15-1/2 by 10-1/2 inch jelly roll pan. Combine margarine, oil, chocolate and 1 cup water in a saucepan and heat until chocolate is melted. Combine flour, baking soda, sugar, milk, eggs, cinnamon and vanilla in a large bowl; then combine with chocolate mixture. Pour batter into prepared pan. Bake for 20-25 minutes or until surface springs back when gently pressed with fingertip. Frost cake while still warm.

Serves 10-12

MISCELLANEOUS

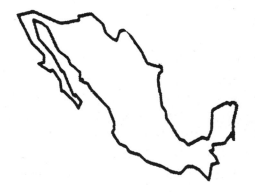

Goat Milk Cheese

Queso de Cabra

1 gallon fresh, whole goat's milk
1 rennet tablet

Add the crushed tablet to warm milk. Allow to stand until a "clabber" has formed. After stirring, place in a cheesecloth bag and allow the whey to drain. Mold into a flat cake. Serve with corn tortillas and hot sauce of choice.

Yield: 2 cups

Purslane

Verdolagas

Fresh purslane*
Mushrooms
Diced onion
Seasoning of choice

Wash purslane thoroughly and dice or tear into small pieces. Saute onion and preferred seasonings. Add mushrooms and saute until tender. Add purslane and cover. Simmer, mixing periodically, for about 15 minutes.

*Purslane is a wild, but edible weed.

Jalapeno Jelly

1/2 cup red bell pepper, seeded and chopped
1/2 cup green bell pepper, seeded and chopped
1/2 cup jalapeno peppers, seeded and finely chopped
6 1/2 cups sugar
1 1/2 cups cider vinegar
1 bottle pectin (equal to one box of two packages)
Green food coloring

Combine everything except pectin. Boil for one minute. Remove from heat and cool for five minutes. Add pectin and stir occasionally to keep peppers in suspension. Add 3-4 drops of green food coloring. Pour into jars. Seal with paraffin while hot. Serve as a condiment for meat.

Yield: 8 cups

Jalapeno Pepper Jelly

4 cups sugar
3/4 cup white vinegar
3 large green peppers
2-3 teaspoons jalapeno peppers, seeded
4 dashes hot sauce
3 ounces liquid pectin
Green food coloring

In blender, puree green peppers. Strain liquid, reserving 1-1/2 cups of pureed green pepper. Puree seeded jalapeno peppers, using 2 or 3 teaspoons depending on how hot jelly is desired. Mix sugar, vinegar, green pepper and jalapeno pepper. Cover with waxed paper and microwave on high for 10-12 minutes or until mixture comes to a rolling boil, stirring twice. Remove waxed paper, reduce power to medium high and boil vigorously for 3 minutes. Add pectin; bring to a rolling boil on high for 1-2 minutes. Reduce to medium high and boil 2 minutes. Add food coloring, skim and pour into four 8 ounce jelly jars; seal. If clear jelly is desired, strain before pouring into jelly jars. Cool at room temperature, then refrigerate.

Microwave oven instructions: 17 minutes to make four (8 ounce) jars.

Yield: 5 cups

Tuna Jelly (Cactus Juice)

2 cups juice from cactus fruit
3 cups sugar
1/2 lemon
2 cups pectin

Wear heavy (leather) gloves to gather cactus fruit. Rub off cactus thorns with a heavy brush. Cut off blossom end. Wash well. Cut cactus in small pieces and cover with water. Cook for 15-20 minutes. Mash and strain through a sieve. Add 1 package of pectin to 2 cups of cactus juice. Cook, stirring constantly until pectin powder is dissolved. Add 3 cups of sugar and continue boiling until mixture forms a film on a spoon. Squeeze juice of lemon and pour into sterilized jars and seal.

Yield: 2 1/2 cups

Tex-Mex Hominy

Nixtamal

8 slices bacon
1 cup onion, chopped
2 (15 1/2 ounce) cans hominy
1 tablespoon all purpose flour
2 large tomatoes, peeled and chopped
1 cup shredded Cheddar cheese, divided
1 teaspoon chili powder
1/4 teaspoon salt
1/4 teaspoon pepper

Cook bacon in a large skillet until crisp; remove bacon, reserving 2 tablespoons drippings in skillet. Crumble bacon and set aside. Add onion and hominy to drippings in skillet; cook until onion is tender. Combine bacon, flour and tomatoes in a large bowl; add hominy mixture, 3/4 cup cheese and remaining ingredients. Spoon into a lightly greased 2 quart casserole; bake at 350 degrees for 25 minutes. Add remaining 1/4 cup cheese and bake an additional 5 minutes or until cheese melts.

Serves 6-8

Purslane in Green Sauce

Verdolagas en Salsa Verde

Purslane*
4-6 tomatillos, see glossary
Serrano peppers to taste
Slice of onion
Coriander
Lemon juice

Wash purslane thoroughly; dice or tear. Place in boiling water, lower temperature, cover and cook until tender (10-15 minutes). In a blender add *tomatillos*, peppers, onion, coriander and lemon juice. Pour over drained purslane.

*Purslane is a wild, but edible weed.

Serves 2-4

Greens

Quelites

Greens (any acceptable edible greens, i.e.: dandelion, kale,
*   mustard, turnip)*
1 small onion, diced
1/2 cup bouillon or vegetable soup

Cut tender leaves and stems and wash thoroughly. Saute onion; add 1/2 to 1 cup bouillon or vegetable soup. Cook over medium heat 15-20 minutes or until tender.

For variety, add cooked ground beef, bacon bits or cooked chicken.

Serves 2

Flower of the Yucca Plant

Flor de Pita

1/2 pound browned ground beef
2 flowers of the Yucca*
Salt and pepper to taste

Cut blossom from yucca and remove center, yellow stem. Wash thoroughly and tear into small pieces (yellow will make the blossom bitter). Boil or saute, covered, over browned meat.

*This is the blossom of the yucca, which grows wild in South Texas and Mexico.

Serves 2

Indian Cactus

Nopalitos Indios

10-12 cactus pads
2 cups mashed beans
1/2 cup flour
Oil for frying
3 eggs
Salt and pepper to taste
Optional:
Avocado
Tomato

Clean cactus pads. Cook by boiling 15-20 minutes. Let drain. Once dry, spread beans to one side of a cactus pad. Cover with another pad, as a sandwich. Roll in flour and place in beaten egg mixture. Fry in hot oil until golden brown. Garnish with avocado, tomato or preferred vegetable.

Serves 4-5

BEVERAGES

Aztec Punch

1 gallon tequila
12 lemons
Sugar to taste
4 (46 ounce) cans grapefruit juice
2 quarts strong cold black tea
1 1/2 teaspoons ground cinnamon

Mix all ingredients together and let stand for an hour or two to blend. Pour over a block of ice in a punch bowl.

Yield: 3 gallons

Border Buttermilk

1 can frozen pink lemonade
Tequila
8 ice cubes

Put lemonade in a blender with the ice cubes. Fill the empty lemonade can with tequila. Blend well.

Yield: 2 cups

Dorado Cocktail

2 ounces tequila
1 tablespoon honey
1/2 lemon

Shake ingredients well with crushed ice and strain into a cocktail glass. Squeeze lemon. Great color and flavor.

Serves 1

Veracruz Cocktail

1 jigger dark rum
1 jigger French (dry) vermouth
1 jigger pineapple juice

Shake well with crushed ice; strain into a chilled cocktail glass.

Serves 1

Fiesta Pearl

1/3 cup grapefruit juice
1/3 cup lemon juice
1/3 cup grenadine
1 egg white
Crushed ice

Combine all ingredients in a shaker or blender and mix thoroughly. Serve in cocktail glasses with a mint leaf or cherry.

Serves 1

Gutierrez Oyster Shots

2 small raw oysters
4 ounces tomato juice
1/2 green lime
4 shakes of celery salt
3 drops of Worcestershire sauce
2 shakes black pepper
3 drops of hot sauce, to taste
1/2 ounce vodka, to taste

In two large shot glasses, mix all ingredients (divided equally.) Drop in the oyster and enjoy. A salted glass is also an option. This quick and enjoyable drink will certainly entertain and impress any oyster lover!

Serves 2

Kahlua Toreador

1 part Kahlua
2 parts brandy
Crushed ice

Shake vigorously with ice and strain into a cocktail glass.

Serves 1

Margarita

2 ounces tequila
1/2 ounce Cointreau
1/2 lime
Salt

Rub the rim of a cocktail glass with the rind of a lime, then spin it on a plate of salt. Pour tequila, Cointreau and squeeze of lime juice over ice in a bar glass; stir until well chilled and strain into the prepared glass.

If you find the recipe is not sweet enough for you, simply increase the amount of Cointreau; if too sweet, decrease it.

Serves 1

Mexican Cocktail

2 ounces light rum
1/2 ounce kummel
1/2 ounce orange juice
Dash of bitters
Crushed ice

Shake well with ice and strain into a chilled cocktail glass.

Serves 1

Mexican Coffee

4 cups (1 quart) strong black coffee
1 teaspoon cinnamon
Sugar
1/2 cup whipping cream
1/16 teaspoon nutmeg
1/16 teaspoon cinnamon

Heat coffee with cinnamon; sweeten to taste. Pour into small dessert cups. Beat whipping cream to soft peaks with nutmeg and cinnamon and sweeten if desired. Top with whipped cream. Sprinkle each serving lightly with cinnamon and serve with a cinnamon stick for stirring.

Serves 4

Mexican Coffee with Kahlua

6 coffee measures (12 level tablespoons) American coffee
1 quart water
4 tablespoons chocolate syrup
16 ounces (1 pint) milk
1/2 cup heavy cream
2 tablespoons confectioners sugar, sifted
2 tablespoons cocoa
1/2 teaspoon vanilla
3 ounces Kahlua

Brew coffee and water. In saucepan, stir chocolate syrup into milk. Slowly bring to a boil. Combine coffee and milk, blending well. Keep warm until serving time. Pour cream, sugar and cocoa into pre-chilled narrow bowl. Beat until thick. Stir in vanilla. Pour coffee into mugs holding at least 8 ounces. Spoon whipped cream on top. Pour 1/2 ounce Kahlua over whipped cream in each mug.

Serves 4-6

Picador Cocktail

1 part Kahlua
2 parts tequila
1 lemon
Crushed ice

Stir well with ice, strain into a cocktail glass and serve it with a twist of lemon.

Serves 1

Mexican Grasshopper

1 part Kahlua
1 part green creme de menthe
1 part cream
Crushed ice

Whirl in the blender with crushed ice and serve in a cocktail glass.

Serves 1

Pancho Villa Cocktail

1 ounce light rum
1 ounce apricot brandy
1 ounce dry gin
1 teaspoon pineapple juice
1 teaspoon cherry brandy

Shake well with shaved ice and serve in a champagne glass. This drink has a high alcohol content. Ingredients may be reduced for individual taste..

Serves 1

Eggnog

Rompope

1 quart milk
1/2 pound sugar
1 vanilla bean
8 egg yolks
1 pint light rum

(In Mexico there is a wooden paddle made for beating, but a modern eggbeater does very well.)

Bring the milk to a boil; let it cool, add the sugar and vanilla bean, return to the fire and let simmer for 20 minutes. Beat the egg yolks thoroughly. Let the milk and sugar mixture cool, remove the vanilla bean, then little by little beat it and the rum into the egg yolks. Let the mixture sit overnight, then put into a bottle and cork tightly. It should be kept for several days before drinking. Serve in small liquer glasses.

This curious Mexican drink is a sort of eggnog, cooked so that it keeps indefinitely. Although it is made commercially and sold in liquor stores, many people make it at home. Most recipes call for pure alcohol, which is obtainable in Mexico at a low price, but rum may be used advantageously.

Serves 6

Tequila Cocktail

2 ounces tequila
1 ounce dry vermouth
Few drops vanilla extract

Stir with ice and strain into a chilled cocktail glass.

As you can see, except for the vanilla, this is pretty much like a tequila Martini (Tequini). As a matter of fact, tequila is a fine substitute for gin in many drinks. Its slightly peppery quality is a most welcome change. Try your favorite Martini formula using tequila --you will like it and so will your guests. Tequila also makes a fine apertif. Keep a bottle in the freezer or the freezing compartment of the refrigerator. To serve, simply pour the super cold liquor into pre-chilled shot glasses or liquer glasses.

Serves 1

Tequila Daisy

4 ounces tequila
1 ounce lemon juice
1 ounce grenadine
1 ounce club soda

Shake all ingredients well with crushed ice and strain into two chilled cocktail glasses. Pink, pretty and delicious.

Serves 2

Tequila Sunrise

2 ounces tequila
3 dashes grenadine
Juice and peel of 1/2 lime
1/2 teaspoon creme de cassis
Club soda

Put first four ingredients into a sour or highball glass with several ice cubes. Add club soda to fill and stir on the rocks.

Serves 1

Tequila Sour

1/2 lemon
1 teaspoon sugar
Dash of Angostura bitters
Club soda
Crushed ice
Optional:
1 egg white

Shake the first four ingredients well with ice, pour into a sour glass, and add a splash of club soda. Decorate with fruit if you like. Lemon juice and sugar may be juggled to suit your taste, but it should definitely be on the sour side.

Another way of making this is to add an egg white, shake all ingredients vigorously, strain into a Collins glass over ice cubes, and fill with club soda.

Serves 1

Tea Wine

1 quart boiling water
12 teabags
1/2 cup sugar
3 cups dry red wine
2/3 cup strained lemon juice
Lemon wedges
Optional:
Mint sprig

Pour boiling water over teabags; cover and let stand 5 minutes. Remove teabags; add sugar and stir to dissolve. Cool. Add wine and lemon juice. Pour into a tall pitcher; add ice cubes. Garnish with lemon wedges and, if desired, add a mint sprig.

Note: This wine-tea punch may be made with lemon-flavored iced tea mix if desired. Simply add 2 envelopes of the mix to a quart of cold water. Stir to dissolve. Add 3 cups dry red wine and ice cubes.

Serves 10

White Sangria

5 oranges
4 lemons
4 limes
4 cups extra-fine sugar
5-3 liter jugs dry white wine, chilled
2 quarts club soda, chilled

Slice fruit into thin slices. Add sugar and mash slightly. Let stand about 30 minutes. Add wine, soda, and ice if desired. If preparing early, do not add soda until ready to serve.

Serves 30

Xochimilco

Kahlua
Cream

Simply pour Kahlua into a cordial glass and float a thin layer of cream on top. Serve after dinner.

Serves 1

The Orendain Collection

When the KMBH-TV production team was in the state of Jalisco video-taping for **"Mexico: Its People and Places"** and **"Discover Mexico,"** they were given a guided tour of one of the tequila making plants owned by the Orendain family of Tequila, Mexico.

After finding out that the station was developing a series on Mexican cuisine, Mr. Eduardo Orendain, the Mayor of Tequila and a distiller, was gracious enough to provide us with his family's personal recipes for Mexico's most famous drink.

Orendain Batanga

1 1/2 ounce Ollitas Orendain Tequila or White Tequila
1 1/4 teaspoon fresh lemon juice
6 ounces cola
Salt

Frost a large glass. In a saucer, add salt and twirl rim of glass in it. Pour all ingredients over ice in the salt-rimmed glass and stir.

Serves 1

Orendain Margarita

1 1/4 ounce White Orendain Tequila
1/2 ounce fresh lemon juice
3/4 Cointrau
Salt
Crushed ice

Frost a large glass with salt and add ice. Mix the ingredients in a cocktail shaker and strain into glass.

Serves 1

Orendain Pina Colada

1 1/2 White Orendain Tequila
1/4 ounce coconut cream
2 ounces pineapple juice
Crushed ice

Mix all ingredients and decorate with pineapple or cherry.

Serves 1

Orendain Puerto Vallarta

1 1/2 ounce White Orendain Tequila
1/4 ounce fresh lemon juice
1/4 grenadine, sweet mix
6 ounces orange juice

In a cocktail shaker mix all ingredients and strain into a large glass with ice. Decorate with a slice of orange, lemon or cherry.

Serves 1

Orendain Vampiro

1 1/2 Tequila Orendain Blanco
6 ounces sangrita

In a frosted, salted glass, add ice and ingredients.

Serves 1

Silk Stockings Orendain

1 ounce White Tequila Orendain
1 1/3 ounce evaporated milk
1/2 ounce liquor of cacao
1/3 ounce condensed sweet milk
1/3 ounce sweet liquor grenadine
Crushed ice

Mix all ingredients in a tall glass. Decorate with a cherry.

Serves 1

Sunrise Orendain

1 1/2 ounce White Orendain Tequila
1/3 ounce sweet mix grenadine
6 ounces grapefruit juice
Crushed ice

Mix all ingredients in a tall glass.

Serves 1

Sunset Orendain

1 1/2 ounces Orendain Crema de Almendrado
6 ounces orange juice
Crushed ice

Mix all ingredients in a tall glass. Decorate with cherry or lemon slice.

Serves 1

GLOSSARY

Atole--A pre-Hispanic drink or porridge made with masa, raw sugar, and crushed fruits for flavor.

Bunuelo--Tortilla dough, rolled out and fried. Sugar and cinnamon can be added.

Burritos--A flour tortilla rolled around a filling and fried.

Caldo-- The Spanish word for broth or soup.

Carnes--The Spanish word for meats.

Carnitas--Small fried pieces of meat pickled for tacos that serves as a snack.

Ceviche--Fish marinated in lime juice and/or vinegar.

Chalupa--A round, fried corn tortilla on which toppings are placed.

Chilaquiles--Made by cutting corn tortillas into small pieces, frying them, and serving in a chili sauce and broth.

Chile--Types of peppers in this book: *mulato, ancho, pequin, jalapeno, poblano, serrano, cascabel, pasilla, and habanero.*

Chorizo--A spicy Mexican sausage.

Cilantro--The green leafy seasoning, often called coriander. Looks like parsley, but has a very different taste.

Comal--A round, cast iron griddle used to make or warm tortillas.

Elote--An ear of corn.

Enchilada--A tortilla dipped in sauce and rolled around cheese and/or meat.

Epazote--Referred to as goosefoot in this book. It is a strong herb that is used for cooking and medicinal purposes.

Fajita--A Tex-Mex entree made of barbequed beef skirt wrapped in a flour or corn tortilla.

Frijoles--Beans, whether pinto, black or red. These can also be "*a la-charra*" which means cooked in their broth.

Goosefoot--The Spanish word is *epazote*. A strong herb that is used for cooking and medicinal purposes.

Guachinango--Can also be spelled *huachinango*. Sea fish, it is almost red when alive. When cooked, its color disappears.

Gordita--A corn tortilla made with lard or shortening, smaller and thicker than a regular corn tortilla, and may also be made with sugar.

Jicama--A white bulb resembling an onion that grows throughout Mexico and Central America. It has a sweet and watery taste.

Masa de harina--Dough made from ground, dried corn and water. It is the basic ingredient of corn tortillas and tamales.

Mole--A spicy sauce used most often on fowl and commonly made with either chocolate or peanut butter. Pronounced "mo-Lay".

Nopal--The Prickly Pear cactus, parts of which are edible.

Pepitas--Spanish for shelled pumpkin seeds.

Quesadilla--A fried tortilla turnover with a filling.

Peppers--See *chile*.

Rajas--Means a strip of something, usually a pepper.

Relleno--Spanish for stuffing or filling, such as cheese.

Sopa--Spanish for soup. It can also be a method of cooking. For example, *sopa de arroz* is Mexican rice, but certainly not a soup or "soupy".

Taco or taquito--A corn or flour tortilla wrapped around a filling.

Tamal(e)--Made from corn dough and lard, wrapped in a husk and filled with shredded meat and steamed.

Tomatillos--Green and smaller than regular tomatoes, but not unripe, they are all together separate plants. Encased in husks when fresh, they are also available canned.

Tortilla--A flat corn or flour bread made round and cooked on a comal.

Tostada--A tortilla fried crispy. If a topping is put on it, it is a chalupa.

Tuna--The fruit of the nopal or cactus. It is used mainly in fruit salads.

Verdolaga--Purslane, an annual herbaceous plant, its stems are large, thick, and juicy. It is an orchard plant used as a vegetable.

SPECIAL ACKNOWLEDGEMENTS

THE MEXICAN KITCHEN with Rod Santana was over two years in the making and went through many, many revisions and reviews. Many of the original submissions came from the Zonta Club of Harlingen, Texas. Added to that core of recipes were the submission of many other individuals who live in the Lower Rio Grande Valley of South Texas.

Still other recipes were added into the mix through research. In the final reviews, very few of the original recipes survived in exactly the form they were submitted.

The recipes here are predominately a merger of the work of a great many fantastic cooks who worked with Jozi Maldonado, the Co-Executive Producer of the companion television series, and host Rod Santana to publish a work that truly reflects recipes from our part of the world.

A special debt is owed to our Editorial Review Committee who worked with the TV station in choosing recipes: Mrs. Juanita Elizondo Garza of Edinburg; Mr. Jim Wilson of Edinburg; Mr. and Mrs. Luis C. Gutierrez of Harlingen; and KMBH's Jozi Maldonado of Raymondville.

Two very special people, Linn Keller of the Rio Grande Valley Museum and Anne Glenn from Adventures In Travel, were kind enough to donate their time and assist us with the final proofing of the book. Mrs. Elva Garcia also helped in editing and selecting recipes. Virtually every staff member of KMBH-TV also contributed to this project.

The following people were gracious enough to submit recipies to this collection. Without their assistance, we could not have published a cookbook or produced a television series.

Alice
Domitila Vela
Baytown
Delia Villarreal

Brownsville
Alicia Martinez
Delbert Runyon

Combes
Mary Bowen

Edinburg
Juanita Garza
Jim Wilson

Harlingen
Nancy Ashcraft
Alma Bassett
Dorothea Beller
Judy Brady
Von Brookshire
Rosemary
    Courtney
Carol Daiser
Mary Day
Noel Duran
Norma Ellington
Tillie Elizalde
Katherine Fairfield
Elizabeth Garrett
Yolanda Gonzales
Patricia Guillermo
Luis Gutierrez
Kaye Kinninmouth

Eleanor King
Brenda Krafk
Eudora Lawrence
Hilda Leal
Nino Lucio
Karyn Mason
Carolyn McCarley
Betty McCune
Trudy McGinnis
Adelene McGee
Margaret Mitchell
Francis Morris
Angela Murray
Erika Perez
Lydia Perez
Peggy Perez
Karen Potter
Angie Ramirez
Augelita Ramirez
Conchita Reyes
Judy Riley
Candy Rios
Virginia Sletner
Catherine Snider
Mary Lee Spillman
June Sportman
Alicia Valdez
Oralia Young
    Freda Hale
    Thelma Harbin
La Feria
    Lois Edmonds

McAllen
Evelyn Anne Greenhill

Mercedes
Colleen Ferguson

Raymondville
Atanacia
    Maldonado
Jozi Maldonado
Ida Nora Vargas

Rio Hondo
Juanity Brodecky
Oralia Uresti

San Benito
Thelma Bohner
Margaret Brown
Tad Brown
Annette Dillard
Dana Norman

South Padre Island
Shirley Goodman